THE
HUNGRY
STUDENT
VEGETARIAN
COOKBOOK

MORE THAN 200 QUICK
AND SIMPLE RECIPES

hamlyn

hamlyn

First published in Great Britain in 2015 by Spruce,
This edition published by Hamlyn,
a division of Octopus Publishing Group Ltd
Carmelite House, 50 Victoria Embankment
London EC4Y 0DZ
www.octopusbooksusa.com

An Hachette UK Company
www.hachette.co.uk

Copyright © Octopus Publishing Group Ltd 2015, 2023

Distributed in the US by Hachette Book Group
1290 Avenue of the Americas
4th and 5th Floors, New York, NY 10104

Distributed in Canada by Canadian Manda Group
664 Annette St, Toronto, Ontario, Canada M6S 2C8

ISBN 978-0-600-63787-5

Printed and bound in China

10 9 8 7 6 5 4 3 2 1

Drinking excessive alcohol can significantly damage your
health. The US Department of Health and Human Sciences
recommends men do not regularly exceed 1–2 drinks a day and
women 1 drink. Never operate a vehicle when you have been
drinking alcohol. Octopus Publishing Group accepts no liability
or responsibility for any consequences resulting from the
use of or reliance upon the information contained herein.

This book includes dishes made with nuts and nut
derivatives. Standard level spoon measurements are
used throughout. Ovens should be preheated to the
specified temperature— if using a fan-assisted oven,
follow the manufacturer's instructions for adjusting the
time and the temperature.

CONTENTS

INTRODUCTION

Leaving home is both an exciting and daunting prospect. Although you probably feel ready to move out and gain your independence, there's a lot to be said for clothes that miraculously get washed and ironed, a refrigerator full of fresh food, and plates that don't require week-old takeout to be chiseled off before they can be used. And then there's the big issue of cooking for yourself—something you will have to master quickly unless you are resigned to three years of cereal and toast.

If kitchen appliances and cooking techniques are alien concepts, don't worry—a few key skills and a handful of reliable recipes are all you need to be sure you don't die of boredom at mealtimes. Even the most inexperienced cook can learn how to rustle up a quick pasta dinner or do something creative with eggs. If nothing else, necessity will generally help you to overcome any kitchen phobias; if no one else will be cooking your dinner, you'll have to roll up your sleeves and cook it yourself.

BUDGETING

It might be dull but good budgeting will get you through college without going into serious debt. When it comes to food, you'll discover that you can actually enjoy a more varied and healthy diet by shopping sensibly and cooking your own meals than by handing your weekly food allowance over the counter at a fast-food outlet or convenience store.

If you're living with friends, you can save a fortune by organizing a communal food budget. It means you can take advantage of bulk-buy deals and food that's coming close to its expiration date and being sold at a discount. A household budget also means you can take turns to do the weekly shopping and to prepare meals, so you can all enjoy home-cooked food every night without having to spend too much time in the kitchen. If you're really organized, you could work out a weekly meal plan and shopping list, which will save time and money when at the supermarket.

When you're working out a budget, you need to take your total weekly living allowance into account. Deduct set expenditure, such as rent, utility bills, and travel expenses, then the amount you're left with can be divided between your shopping basket and entertaining. Older students of legal drinking age may also need to allow for alcohol in their budget.

If you are a vegetarian in a meat-eating household, you will need to make sure you include a good variety of beans and other legumes, such as lentils, and vegetables on the shopping list if it's not your turn to visit the supermarket—carnivores might automatically head for the meat aisles for their protein fix and could need a nudge to push the shopping cart over to the beans.

SHARING

If you are from a big family, you should be used to sharing, but this probably doesn't extend to food. The first time your special block of cheese or slice of cake disappears from the refrigerator may be a shock, but this is something you need to get used to. No matter how close you are to your pals, there will be a time when munchies or late-night desperation will lead them to taking whatever culinary treats are on hand.

It makes sense to put a few house rules in place when you first move in. If you're shopping as a household, you need to be clear about whether this is for the ingredients for all your meals, or just household basics, such as bread and milk. If anyone wants something additional, they should pay for it themselves—but that also means it's out of bounds. Obviously, there will be a few blurred lines if you have one communal refrigerator and the kitchen cabinets are a household free-for-all. Again, you need to decide if you going to have some individual space for your own food, or whether you trust everyone to stick to the rules and keep their hands off the exotic fruit platter that you've been looking forward to eating all day.

Milk, bread, and other essentials will need to be bought more often than the weekly shopping, so it's a good idea to have a separate money pot for them, and take it in turns to buy them. You could all put a few dollars a week into a pot to cover the cost, and any leftover money can be added to the food budget to buy a few treats.

STAY HEALTHY

Kitchens are breeding grounds for a number of nasty bugs, and the combination of living in close proximity to other people and the student aversion to washing dishes means there's more of a chance you'll fall prey to them. It only takes a few minutes a day to wipe kitchen surfaces with antibacterial spray and, if the luxury of a dishwasher has evaded you, the same goes for washing dishes. A cleaning rota can help to solve the problem of certain people dodging their housekeeping duties. Put it somewhere prominent so the culprits can be named and shamed, but also make it realistic; if some people have a fear of mopping floors but are unfazed by dusting, then allocate tasks among your housemates accordingly.

A clean kitchen will definitely lower your chances of a stopover in hospital, but you also need to be careful when handling and preparing food. Vegetarians have a natural advantage here, because many cases of food poisoning and other food-related illnesses are linked to raw meat contaminating other foods, or not cooking meat properly. However, you're not off the hook.

- **COVER UP** Uncovered food will attract flies; always keep food covered or stored in the refrigerator. The same goes for trash cans: empty them once they're full; don't try and squeeze more garbage in.

- **FRUIT BATH** Always thoroughly rinse fruit and vegetables before you eat or cook with them. You don't know how many other people have handled them before they reached your kitchen.

- **FURRY FRIENDS** Mice (and insects) love spilled food, overflowing trash cans, and leftovers left out. The problem is, so do a lot of students...

- **STRANGE SMELLS** If an ingredient smells strange, chances are it's bad and shouldn't be eaten. If you pick up a bargain at the supermarket that's on its last day for being eaten, stick to the advice and eat it that day.

KITCHEN EQUIPMENT

You need to accept that your kitchen won't be decked out like a showroom and you will probably have to make do with limited storage and preparation space. You will also be relying on donations of kitchen equipment from your family, or bargain-basement sets of dinnerware and pans.

However, you don't need to be equipped like a celebrity chef to create good-quality meals. Choose your implements wisely and—as long as the oven works—you'll be able to put together the recipes in this book with the minimum equipment. Here are some basics you'll need to get you started.

Utensils Measuring cups and spoons, liquid measuring cup, two mixing bowls of different sizes, wooden spoon, rolling pin, grater, spatula, cutting board, vegetable peeler, whisk, colander, sharp knives (one small for prepping veg and one large for chopping, slicing bread, etc.).

Pots and pans Large and small saucepan (with lids), large nonstick skillet, steamer (useful but a metal colander over a pan will work fine). A wok is handy but not essential.

Cookware Baking sheet, roasting pan, flameproof casserole dish, large rectangular ovenproof dish (for lasagnes, baked goods, etc.), wire cooling rack, cake pans, muffin pan, and pastry cutters (if you're a baker).

An immersion blender is ideal for blending soups or making smoothies, but if there's an extra food processor hanging around at the family home, it would be a good addition to your kitchen. They're great for chopping large quantities of vegetables and making sauces and cakes. They can also be used to juice fresh fruit.

Obviously, if you have a particular penchant for Spanish food or homemade bread, you'll probably want to pack a paella dish or your collection of loaf pans in your luggage. There's an almost endless list of kitchen implements and gadgets for every possible ingredient and preparation technique. But as long as you have the basics, you'll eat well.

If you know your housemates, it's a good idea to make a list of everything you will need and then divide it up. There's no point moving in and discovering that all four of you have brought citrus parers but you don't have a saucepan between you. The same goes for dinnerware—you don't all need to bring a full set of plates, bowls, and glasses. Apart from taking up valuable kitchen space, the more of these there are to use, the less often the dishes will be washed—and the larger the stack of dirty dishes will get.

ESSENTIAL INGREDIENTS

Whether you turn up on your first day with armfuls of food or you sit down with your housemates and plan your first week's shopping, there are certain ingredients that you'll use time and again and you'll need to keep in the cupboards.

Condiments Salt and black pepper are the mainstays of many recipes and good seasoning will lift an ordinary dish up to the next dimension. You will also need vegetable oil for cooking and olive oil for dressings and sauces. Vegetable bouillon cubes are another mainstay, but you can also make your own broth from scratch (see page 246). Ketchup, mayonnaise, and mustard should also be present in any student kitchen.

Butter Toast is a student staple, so a good supply of butter or margarine is essential. It is also essential for good mashed potatoes.

Spices You don't need a huge variety of spices but a few essentials, such as curry powder, cumin seeds, paprika, or turmeric, will add depth and heat to dishes. If using store-bought pastes, check the labels to make sure they are suitable for vegetarians.

Onions and garlic From Mexican and Italian dishes to Indian curries, these two ingredients are essential to the success of so many dishes; always keep a ready supply.

Dried pasta and rice Both have a long shelf life, are extremely versatile, and provide you with a good source of carbohydrates. Don't go too crazy with the pasta shapes; stick to a couple of favourites—and choose whole wheat for a healthier option.

Cans Cans of beans (kidney beans, black beans, pinto beans and lima beans, as well as baked beans), corn kernels, chickpeas (garbanzo beans), and diced tomatoes are great staples when the budget is tight. They are cheap and can be used to bulk up soups, stews, and casseroles or added to salads.

Freezer staples Depending on space, it's a good idea to keep an extra loaf of bread tucked away for emergency breakfasts. A few bags of frozen vegetables could also get you out of a tight spot, while bumper crops of seasonal fruit, such as blueberries, strawberries, raspberries, or plums (halved and with the pits removed), can be frozen and used in smoothies and desserts.

GETTING STARTED

With a litte patience and practice you will soon be enjoying delicious home-cooked meals that don't cost a fortune, and in the following pages you'll find everything you need to guide you through your culinary adventures at college.

BUDGETING

Boring as it may be, unless you want to spend the last month of each semester hiding in your hovel and eating plain rice, budgeting is a necessary part of student life. Each recipe in this book is rated from 1 to 3, with 1s providing end-of-semester saviors that can be scraped together for a pittance, and 3s to splash out and impress all your friends.

Bring on breakfast

HASH BROWNS WITH FRIED EGGS

BUCKWHEAT CREPES

BLUEBERRY & LEMON
PANCAKES

PESTO SCRAMBLED EGGS

HONEY-ROASTED GRANOLA

Berry & HONEY YOGURTS

1 Using an immerion blender or a food processor or blender, if you have one, blend half the berries with the orange juice and honey until smooth. Transfer to a bowl and stir in the remaining berries.

2 Divide one-third of the berry mixture among four glasses or small bowls. Top with half the yogurt. Layer with half the remaining berry mixture and top with the remaining yogurt.

3 Top with the remaining berry mixture and sprinkle the granola over the top just before serving.

3½ cups frozen mixed berries
  (thawed)
juice of 1 orange
⅓ cup honey
1¾ cups vanilla yogurt
½ cup granola

Serves **4**
Prep time **10 minutes**

AFFORDABILITY
2

PUMPKIN SEED & APRICOT MUESLI

IF YOU'RE NOT A MORNING PERSON, MAKE THIS MUESLI THE NIGHT BEFORE. FOLLOW STEP 1 AND PUT THE MIXTURE IN THE REFRIGERATOR OVERNIGHT. THE NEXT MORNING, ADD THE APPLES AND MILK. THIS WILL ALSO PRODUCE A SOFTER-TEXTURED MUESLI.

½ cup rolled oats
1 tablespoon golden raisins
   or raisins
1 tablespoon pumpkin or
   sunflower seeds
1 tablespoon chopped almonds
3 tablespoons chopped
   dried apricots
2 tablespoons orange or
   apple juice
2 small sweet, crisp apples,
   peeled and grated
3 tablespoons soy milk or milk

Serves **2**
Prep time **10 minutes**

1 Put the oats, golden raisins or raisins, seeds, almonds, and apricots into a bowl with the fruit juice.

2 Add the grated apples and stir to mix. Top with your chosen milk and serve.

STUDENT TIP

Take a calculator to the supermarket (or use your Smartphone). Adding up prices as you add food to the shopping cart is a good way to shop within your budget and make informed choices about what you buy.

AFFORDABILITY
1

HONEY-ROASTED
G R A N O L A

⅓ cup honey
2 tablespoons vegetable oil
3 cups rolled oats
½ cup coarsely chopped
   hazelnuts
½ cup blanched almonds,
   coarsely chopped
⅓ cup dried cranberries
⅓ cup dried blueberries

To serve
milk or yogurt
fresh fruit (optional)

Serves **4**
Prep time **10 minutes,**
plus cooling
Cooking time **25-30 minutes**

1 Heat the honey and oil together gently in a small saucepan. Mix the oats and nuts together thoroughly in a large bowl. Pour over the warm honey mixture and stir well to combine.

2 Spread the mixture over a large nonstick baking sheet and bake in a preheated oven, at 300°F, for 20-25 minutes, stirring once, until golden.

3 Let the granola cool, then stir in the dried berries. Serve with milk or yogurt and fresh fruit, if desired. Any remaining granola can be stored in an airtight container.

AFFORDABILITY
2

Quinoa Porridge
WITH RASPBERRIES

1 Bring the milk to a boil in a small saucepan, add the quinoa, and return to a boil. Reduce the heat to low, cover with a lid, and simmer for about 15 minutes, until three-quarters of the milk has been absorbed.

2 Stir the sugar and cinnamon into the pan, replace the lid, and cook for 8-10 minutes or until almost all the milk has been absorbed and the quinoa is tender.

3 Spoon the porridge into bowls, then top with the raspberries, sprinkle with the seeds, and drizzle with the honey. Serve immediately.

2½ cups milk
½ cup quinoa
2 tablespoons sugar
½ teaspoon ground cinnamon
1 cup fresh raspberries
2 tablespoons mixed seeds, such as sunflower, flaxeed, pumpkin, and hemp seeds
2 tablespoons honey

Serves **2**
Prep time **5 minutes**
Cooking time **25-30 minutes**

AFFORDABILITY
1

BLUEBERRY & LEMON *Pancakes*

1 cup all-purpose flour
2 teaspoons baking powder
finely grated zest of ½ lemon
1 tablespoon sugar
1 egg, lightly beaten
1 tablespoon lemon juice
²/₃ cup low-fat milk
1 cup blueberries
vegetable oil, for frying

To serve
butter
preserves or jelly

Serves **4**
Prep time **10 minutes**
Cooking time **20 minutes**

1 Sift the flour and baking powder into a bowl and stir in the lemon zest and sugar. Add the egg and lemon juice and gradually whisk in the milk to make a smooth, thick batter. Stir in the blueberries.

2 Heat a large nonstick skillet and rub it with a piece of paper towel drizzled with a little oil. Drop spoonfuls of the batter, spaced well apart, in the pan and cook for 2–3 minutes, until bubbles form on the surface and the underside is golden brown, then turn the pancakes over and cook on the other side. Wrap in a clean dish towel and keep warm while cooking the remaining batter in the same way.

AFFORDABILITY
1

BUCKWHEAT CREPES

1 Sift the flours into a bowl and add the grains left in the sifter. Beat the egg and milk together in a small bowl, then slowly add to the flour. Stir until a smooth batter forms. If the batter is a little thick, add a little more milk. Let stand for 20 minutes, then stir again.

2 Put 1 teaspoon of the oil in a nonstick skillet. When it's hot, add 2 tablespoons of the pancake batter and shake the pan so it spreads. Cook for 2 minutes, until the underside is lightly browned, then turn the pancake over and cook on the other side for a minute or so. Transfer to a plate and keep warm in a low oven while cooking the remaining batter in the same way.

½ cup whole wheat flour
½ cup buckwheat flour
1 egg
1¼ cups skim milk
8 teaspoons olive oil

To serve
fresh fruit
plain yogurt

Serves **4**
Prep time **5 minutes,
plus standing**
Cooking time **25 minutes**

AFFORDABILITY **1**

Tomato & Bell Pepper
TORTILLAS

1 tablespoon vegetable oil
1 small onion, finely chopped
1 garlic clove, crushed
1 mild green chile, seeded and
   finely chopped
1 small green bell pepper,
   cored, seeded, and thinly
   sliced
1 small red bell pepper, cored,
   seeded, and thinly sliced
1 (14½ oz) can diced tomatoes
2 tablespoons ketchup
4 eggs
4 corn tortillas
smoked paprika, for sprinkling
salt and black pepper

Serves **4**
Prep time **15 minutes**
Cooking time **25-30 minutes**

1 Heat the oil in a large skillet with a lid, add the onion, garlic, chile, and bell peppers, and cook over medium heat for 10-15 minutes, stirring frequently, until the bell peppers are soft. Stir in the tomatoes and ketchup and season with salt and black pepper. Bring to a boil, then reduce the heat and simmer for 5 minutes, until thickened.

2 Make four shallow hollows in the tomato mixture with the back of a spoon and break an egg into each hollow. Cover the pan and cook over low heat for about 5 minutes, until just set.

3 Meanwhile, warm the tortillas according to the package directions. Place each tortilla on a warm serving plate and carefully transfer the egg-and-tomato mixture onto each tortilla. Serve immediately, sprinkled with a little smoked paprika.

AFFORDABILITY 1

Pesto
SCRAMBLED EGGS

12 eggs
½ cup light cream or milk
2 tablespoons butter
4 slices of whole-grain
  bread, toasted
¼ cup pesto, homemade (see
  page 249) or store-bought
salt and black pepper

Serves **4**
Prep time **5 minutes**
Cooking time **5 minutes**

1 Beat together the eggs, cream or milk, and a little salt and black pepper in a bowl. Melt the butter in a large nonstick skillet, add the egg mixture, and stir over low heat with a wooden spoon until cooked to your preference.

2 Put each slice of toast on a warm serving plate. Spoon one-quarter of the scrambled eggs onto each slice of toast, make a small indent in the center, and add a tablespoonful of pesto. Serve immediately.

SHOPPING
ON A BUDGET

When you're on a tight budget, food can often get pushed down the list of priorities. With studying, sleeping, and social events taking up the majority of your time, it can be difficult to find any extra hours in the day to shop around for good-value, good-quality food. However, it's worth spending a little time hunting for some culinary bargains—you'll save money and also add more variety to your diet.

ONLINE CHECKOUT

Shopping online is a good way to stick rigidly to a shopping list, because the enticing advertisements in the supermarket are safely out of reach. You will see exactly how much you're spending as you fill your basket and can quickly delete items if you need to rein in your budget before you check out. While most supermarkets charge for delivery, it could still work out cheaper than getting the bus or paying for parking, and you'll often find that daytime slots cost less, which is perfect for students.

MARKETS

While it's true that many of the gourmet delights offered at local farmers' markets might be beyond your limited means, seasonal fruit and vegetables can work out a lot cheaper than those purchased at supermarkets.If you can hold out until the market is about to close, you can get even more for your money, as stall holders try to sell off produce with a shorter shelf life.

POOLING RESOURCES

For certain foods, it works out cheaper to buy in bulk, so it might be worth setting up a weekly food budget with your housemates and shopping together. Long-life ingredients, such as pasta, rice, breakfast cereals, and canned goods are all cheaper in larger quantities, so it makes sense to stock up your shelves and take advantage of supermarket deals. If you're really organized, you could also work out a cooking rota, which means everyone can enjoy home-cooked meals without having to cook every night.

MENU PLANNER

Don't worry, this doesn't have to be a sophisticated, interactive spreadsheet; a few ideas written down on a paper will be fine. It's common knowledge that if you shop for meals with a list, you'll spend less and waste less than if you wander the aisles picking up random ingredients with no recipes in mind.

HASH BROWNS
WITH FRIED EGGS

● ●

1 Using a grater, coarsely grate the potatoes. Wrap in a clean dish towel and squeeze out the excess liquid over the sink. Transfer to a bowl and stir in the onion, rosemary, and salt and black pepper.

2 Heat half the oil in a large skillet. Divide the potato mixture into quarters and spoon into four 5 inch mounds in the pan, pressing down to form patties. Cook over medium heat for 5 minutes on each side, until cooked through, then transfer to warm serving plates and keep warm in a moderate oven.

3 Heat the remaining oil in the skillet for about 1 minute, until hot, add the eggs, two at a time, and fry until the whites are bubbly and crisp. Serve the eggs on the hash browns, garnished with chopped parsley.

6 russet or Yukon gold potatoes, peeled
1 onion, thinly sliced
2 teaspoons chopped rosemary
¼ cup vegetable oil
4 extra-large eggs
salt and black pepper
chopped parsley, to garnish

Serves **4**
Prep time **15 minutes**
Cooking time **15 minutes**

AFFORDABILITY
1

OVEN-BAKED
Sausage Brunch

1 Heat the oil in a nonstick ovenproof dish or roasting dish in a preheated oven, at 400ºF, until hot.

2 Add the sausages and potatoes to the hot oil and turn to coat in the oil. Cook in the oven for 10 minutes.

3 Remove the dish from the oven, add the mushrooms and tomatoes, and turn with the sausages and potatoes to coat in the oil. Return to the oven and cook for another 10-12 minutes, until the potatoes are golden and the sausages are cooked through.

4 Make two separate spaces in the baked mixture and break an egg into each. Return to the oven and cook for another 3-4 minutes, until the eggs are softly set. Grind over some black pepper and serve immediately.

1 tablespoon vegetable oil
4 vegetarian sausages
2 potatoes, scrubbed and cut into ½ inch cubes
4 mini portobello mushrooms, trimmed
2 tomatoes, halved
2 extra-large eggs
black pepper

Serves **2**
Prep time **10 minutes**
Cooking time **30 minutes**

BEAN CASSEROLE

Comfort Food

TOMATO & CHICKPEA STEW

POTATO & ONION PIZZA

LEMON & SPINACH SOUP

HEARTY
Minestrone

3 carrots
1 red onion
6 celery sticks
2 tablespoons vegetable oil
2 garlic cloves, crushed
2 Yukon gold or white round
  potatoes, peeled and cut into
  ½ inch dice
¼ cup tomato paste
6½ cups Vegetable Broth
  (see page 246)
1 (14½ oz) can diced tomatoes
4 oz short soup pasta shapes
1 (15 oz) can cannellini (white
  kidney) beans, drained
3½ cups baby spinach
salt and black pepper
crusty bread, to serve

1 Finely chop the carrots, onion, and celery. (You can do this in a food processor or blender, if you have one, but coarsely chop the vegetables before adding them to the machine.)

2 Heat the oil in a large saucepan, add the chopped vegetables, garlic, potatoes, tomato paste, broth, tomatoes, and pasta. Bring to a boil, then reduce the heat, cover with a lid, and simmer for 12–15 minutes.

3 Add the cannellini beans and spinach for the final 2 minutes of cooking time. Season to taste and serve with crusty bread.

Serves **4**
Prep time **15 minutes**
Cooking time **15-20 minutes**

AFFORDABILITY
1

CURRIED
Parsnip Soup

1 Heat the butter and oil in a large saucepan, add the chopped onion, garlic, and ginger, and cook over medium heat for 4-5 minutes, until softened. Stir in the curry powder and cumin seeds and cook, stirring, for 2 minutes, then stir in the parsnips, making sure that they are well coated in the spice mixture.

2 Pour in the broth and bring to a boil, then reduce the heat, cover with a lid, and simmer for 20-25 minutes, until the parsnips are tender. Season to taste with salt and black pepper.

3 Blend the soup with an immersion blender until smooth, or transfer to a food processor or blender, in batches, to blend. Reheat gently if necessary.

4 Ladle into warm cups, add dollops of yogurt, and garnish with the cilantro. Serve with warmed naan.

2 tablespoons butter
1 tablespoon vegetable oil
1 onion, chopped
2 garlic cloves, crushed
1 inch piece of fresh ginger root, peeled and chopped
1 tablespoon medium curry powder
1 teaspoon cumin seeds
6 parsnips (about 1½ lb), peeled and chopped
4 cups Vegetable Broth (see page 246)
salt and black pepper

To serve
plain yogurt
2 tablespoons chopped fresh cilantro leaves
naan or other flatbread

Serves **4**
Prep time **15 minutes**
Cooking time **30-35 minutes**

AFFORDABILITY
1

Lima Bean & VEGETABLE SOUP

1 tablespoon vegetable oil
2 teaspoons smoked paprika
1 celery stick, sliced
2 carrots, sliced
1 leek, trimmed and sliced
2½ cups Vegetable Broth
  (see page 246)
1 (14½ oz) can diced tomatoes
1 (15 oz) can lima beans, rinsed
  and drained
2 teaspoons chopped
  rosemary
salt and black pepper
½ cup grated Parmesan-style
  cheese, to serve

Serves 4
Prep time 10 minutes
Cooking time 25 minutes

1 Heat the oil in a large saucepan, add the paprika, celery, carrots, and leek, and cook over medium heat for 3–4 minutes, until the vegetables are slightly softened.

2 Pour in the broth and tomatoes and add the lima beans and rosemary. Season to taste with salt and black pepper and bring to a boil, then reduce the heat, cover with a lid, and simmer for 15 minutes or until the vegetables are just tender.

3 Ladle into warm bowls and sprinkle with the cheese and freshly ground black pepper.

STUDENT TIP
Don't fall into the trap of buying packaged fruit and vegetables. You can save money simply by filling up a bag with loose produce. Next time you go to the supermarket, compare the price per pound of packaged and loose vegetables—you'll never buy plastic-wrapped carrots again.

SPICY LENTIL & *Tomato Soup*

(V)

1¼ cups dried red lentils
1 tablespoon vegetable oil
1 large onion, finely chopped
1 garlic clove, finely chopped
1 celery stick, finely chopped
¾ cup canned diced tomatoes
½ small green chile, seeded and
   finely chopped (optional)
½ teaspoon paprika
½ teaspoon harissa paste
½ teaspoon ground cumin
2½ cups Vegetable Broth
   (see page 246) or water
salt and black pepper
1 tablespoon chopped fresh
   cilantro, to garnish

Serves 4
Prep time 10 minutes
Cooking time 40-50 minutes

1 Put the lentils into a bowl of water. Heat the oil in a large saucepan, add the onion, garlic, and celery, and sauté over low heat until softened.

2 Drain the lentils and add them to the vegetables with the tomatoes. Mix well. Add the chile, if using, paprika, harissa paste, cumin, and broth or water and season with salt and black pepper. Cover with a lid and simmer gently for 30-40 minutes, until the lentils are soft, adding a little more broth or water if the soup gets too thick.

3 Ladle into warm bowls and serve garnished with a little chopped cilantro.

AFFORDABILITY
1

GREEN LENTIL SOUP
with Spiced Butter

SERVE THE SPICY BUTTER SEPARATELY FOR
STIRRING INTO THE SOUP, SO THAT EACH PERSON
CAN "HEAT UP" THEIR OWN SERVING ACCORDING
TO PERSONAL TASTE.

1 Heat the oil in a saucepan, add the onions, and sauté for
3 minutes. Add the bay leaves, lentils, broth, and turmeric.
Bring to a boil, then reduce the heat, cover with a lid, and
simmer for 20 minutes, until the lentils are tender and
turning mushy. Remove and discard the bay leaves.

2 Meanwhile, to prepare the spiced butter, beat the butter
with the garlic, paprika, cumin seeds, and chile and transfer
to a small serving dish.

3 Stir the cilantro into the soup, season to taste with salt and
black pepper, and serve with the spiced butter in a
separate bowl for stirring into the soup.

3 tablespoons vegetable oil
2 onions, sliced
2 bay leaves
1 cup dried green lentils, rinsed
4 cups Vegetable Broth (see
  page 246)
½ teaspoon turmeric
small handful of cilantro leaves,
  coarsely chopped
salt and black pepper

Spiced butter
4 tablespoons salted butter,
  softened
1 large garlic clove, crushed
1 teaspoon paprika
1 teaspoon cumin seeds
1 red chile, seeded and thinly
  sliced

Serves **4**
Prep time **10 minutes**
Cooking time **25 minutes**

NEW POTATO & LEEK SOUP

1 Halve each potato, or cut into ³/₄ inch slices, if large. Halve the leeks lengthwise, then cut across into thin shreds.

2 Melt the butter in a heavy saucepan, add the mustard seeds, onion, garlic, and potatoes, and sauté gently for 5 minutes. Add the broth and nutmeg and bring just to a boil. Reduce the heat, cover with a lid, and simmer gently for about 10 minutes, until the potatoes are just tender.

3 Stir in the leeks and cilantro and cook for another 5 minutes. Season to taste with salt and black pepper and serve with warm bread.

1 lb new potatoes, scrubbed
3 small leeks, trimmed
3 tablespoons butter
1 tablespoon black mustard seeds
1 onion, chopped
1 garlic clove, thinly sliced
4 cups Vegetable Broth (see page 246)
plenty of grated nutmeg
small handful of fresh cilantro, coarsely chopped
salt and black pepper
warm bread, to serve

Serves 4
Prep time **10 minutes**
Cooking time **20 minutes**

2 tablespoons vegetable oil
1 large onion, finely chopped
2 garlic cloves, finely chopped
1 cup long grain white rice,
  rinsed
5 cups Vegetable Broth
  (see page 246)
¼ cup lemon juice
3 extra-large eggs, beaten
4 cups chopped spinach
salt and black pepper
2 tablespoons chopped parsley,
  to garnish
2 tablespoons grated
  Parmesan-style cheese,
  to serve

Serves 4
Prep time 10 minutes
Cooking time 25-30 minutes

Lemon & SPINACH SOUP

1 Heat the oil in a large saucepan or casserole, add the onion and garlic, and cook gently for 7-8 minutes, until softened. Stir in the rice and cook for 1 minute, then pour in the broth. Simmer gently for 12-15 minutes, until the rice is just tender. Remove from the heat.

2 In a small bowl, whisk the lemon juice with the beaten eggs and a pinch of salt. Continue whisking while you add a ladleful of the hot soup in a slow, steady stream, then whisk the egg mixture into the saucepan of soup.

3 Return the saucepan to low heat and continue stirring for 2-3 minutes, until the soup has thickened slightly, being careful to avoid letting it boil. Stir in the chopped spinach and season to taste, then ladle into warm bowls and sprinkle with the chopped parsley. Serve with the grated cheese.

Lentil Dhal
WITH POTATO CHAPATIS

• • • • • • • • • • • • • • • • • •

1½ cups dried black or green
   lentils, rinsed
2 tablespoons vegetable oil
1 onion, chopped
2 garlic cloves, finely chopped
2 tablespoons mild curry paste
   (suitable for vegetarians)
1¼ cups Vegetable Broth
   (see page 246)
2 tomatoes, coarsely chopped
3 tablespoons chopped
   fresh cilantro
1 tablespoon lemon or lime juice
salt and black pepper

Chapatis
4 russet potatoes, peeled
   and cut into chunks
⅓ cup plus 1 tablespoon
   all-purpose or spelt flour,
   plus extra for dusting
2 teaspoons ground cumin
1 teaspoon turmeric
vegetable oil, for frying

Serves 4
Prep time **30 minutes,**
plus cooling
Cooking time **1 hour**

1 For the chapatis, cook the potatoes in a saucepan of salted boiling water for 12–15 minutes, until tender. Drain, return to the saucepan, and mash until smooth. Transfer to a bowl and let cool.

2 Meanwhile, for the dhal, put the lentils into a saucepan, cover with boiling water, and cook for 15 minutes to soften. Drain.

3 Heat the oil in a saucepan, add the onion, and sauté for 5 minutes. Add the garlic and curry paste, stirring to mix. Add the broth, tomatoes, and lentils, cover with a lid, and cook for 15–20 minutes, until thick and pulpy.

4 Meanwhile, beat the flour, spices, and a little black pepper into the potatoes to make a smooth soft dough. Turn out onto a floured surface and divide into eight pieces. Roll out each on a lightly floured surface until about 5 inches in diameter.

5 Put 1 teaspoon oil in a skillet, tilting the pan so the oil coats the bottom. Add a chapati and cook for 1–2 minutes on each side, until lightly browned. Transfer to a plate and keep warm while cooking the remainder in the same way, adding a little more oil if the pan becomes dry. Stir the cilantro and lemon or lime juice into the dhal and serve with the chapatis.

SPICY TEMPEH

8 oz tempeh or tofu, cut into
  ½ inch cubes
3 garlic cloves, crushed
¼ cup peeled and grated fresh
  ginger root
2 onions, coarsely chopped
6 cardamom pods
2 teaspoons cumin seeds
2 teaspoons coriander seeds
3 tablespoons vegetable oil
2 cinnamon sticks
2 bay leaves
6 whole cloves
1 red chile, seeded and chopped
½ teaspoon turmeric
2 (14½ oz) cans diced tomatoes
2 teaspoons sugar
4 Yukon gold potatoes,
  cut into cubes
8 cups trimmed spinach

Serves **4**
Prep time **20 minutes**
Cooking time **30 minutes**

1 Mix the tempeh in a bowl with the garlic and ginger. Using an immersion blender, or a food processor or blender if you have one, blend the onions and 2 tablespoons water to a puree.

2 Lightly crush the cardamom pods with the cumin and coriander with a mortar and pestle. Alternatively, put them in a plastic food bag and crush to a fine powder with the back of a spoon.

3 Heat the oil in a large nonstick saucepan and sauté the crushed spices with the cinnamon, bay leaves, and cloves for 30 seconds. Add the onion puree to the pan and add the chile and turmeric. Cook for 1 minute, then add the tomatoes, sugar, and potatoes and cover with a lid. Simmer gently for 20 minutes, until the potatoes are tender and the sauce is thick. Add the tempeh and cook for another 5 minutes.

4 Add the spinach to the pan, stirring it into the sauce until it starts to wilt. Cook for another 2 minutes or until the spinach is soft and coated with the sauce. Remove and discard the bay leaves. Serve immediately.

THAI
VEGETABLE CURRY

2 tablespoons vegetable oil
2 onions, chopped
2 garlic cloves, crushed
2 tablespoons red Thai
  curry paste (suitable
  for vegetarians)
1¼ cups hot Vegetable Broth
  (see page 246)
1¾ cups coconut milk
2 tablespoons packed light
  brown or granulated sugar
1 ¼ lb new potatoes
2 cups halved green beans
½ cup chopped fresh cilantro
salt and black pepper

To serve
⅓ cup roasted, unsalted
  peanuts, coarsely chopped
boiled jasmine or long grain rice

Serves **3-4**
Prep time **15 minutes**
Cooking time **40 minutes**

1 Heat the oil in a large saucepan, add the onions, and sauté for 5 minutes, until softened. Add the garlic and sauté for another 1 minute.

2 Blend in the curry paste, then the broth, coconut milk, and sugar. Bring to a boil, reduce the heat to a gentle simmer, and stir in the potatoes. Cover and cook gently for 25 minutes, until the potatoes are tender.

3 Add the green beans, cover with a lid, and cook for another 5 minutes, until the beans have softened but retain a little crunch. Stir in the cilantro and season to taste with salt and black pepper. Spoon into warm bowls with the rice and serve sprinkled with the peanuts.

AFFORDABILITY 2

CAULIFLOWER  ⓥ
& SPINACH CURRY
with Potatoes

3 tablespoons vegetable oil
4 Yukon gold potatoes, peeled
and cut into bite-size chunks
1 large onion, coarsely chopped
¼ cup medium curry paste
(suitable for vegetarians)
½ small cauliflower, cut into
chunky florets
1¼ cups Vegetable Broth
(see page 246)
1 cup coconut milk
½ (10 oz) package frozen
spinach, thawed
chopped fresh cilantro, to
garnish (optional)
cooked rice or warm naan or
other flatbread, to serve

Serves 4
Prep time **10 minutes**
Cooking time **25-30 minutes**

1 Heat the oil in a large saucepan, add the potatoes and onion, and cook over medium heat for 5-6 minutes, stirring occasionally, until the vegetables are tinged with color and begin to soften. Stir in the curry paste and cook for 1 minute to cook the spices.

2 Add the cauliflower to the pan and stir to coat before adding the broth and coconut milk. Bring to a boil, then reduce the heat, cover with a lid, and simmer gently for about 15 minutes, stirring occasionally, until the potatoes and cauliflower are tender and the sauce has thickened.

3 Stir in the spinach and cook for another 2-3 minutes, until the spinach and curry are hot. Serve sprinkled with chopped cilantro, if desired, with rice or warm naan.

Chickpea Puree
WITH EGGS & SPICED OIL

SMOOTH CHICKPEA PUREE, TOPPED WITH FRIED EGGS AND SPICY OIL, MAKES A GREAT SNACK AT ANY TIME OF THE DAY. SERVE ANY LEFTOVER PUREE JUST AS YOU WOULD HUMMUS, WITH WARM PITA BREAD.

1 Using an immersion blender, or a food processor or blender if you have one, blend the chickpeas with the garlic, tahini, milk, 2 tablespoons of the oil, 3 teaspoons of the lemon juice, and salt and black pepper until smooth, scraping the mixture from around the sides of the bowl halfway through. Transfer to a small, heavy saucepan and heat through gently for about 3 minutes while preparing the eggs.

2 Heat another tablespoon of the oil in a small skillet and fry the eggs. Pile the chickpea puree onto serving plates and top each mound with an egg.

3 Add the remaining oil and spices to the pan and heat through gently for 1 minute. Season lightly with salt and black pepper and stir in the remaining lemon juice. Pour the sauce over the eggs and serve garnished with cilantro.

1 (15 oz) can chickpeas, rinsed and drained
3 garlic cloves, sliced
¼ cup tahini
¼ cup milk
⅓ cup olive oil
4 teaspoons lemon juice
2 eggs
½ teaspoon each of cumin, coriander, and fennel seeds, lightly crushed
1 teaspoon sesame seeds
¼ teaspoon dried red-pepper flakes
good pinch of turmeric
salt and black pepper
cilantro leaves, to garnish

Serves **2**
Prep time **5 minutes**
Cooking time **10 minutes**

RED BEANS
WITH COCONUT & CASHEWS

(V)

1 Heat the oil in a large saucepan, add the onions and carrots, and sauté for 3 minutes. Add the garlic, bell pepper, and bay leaves and sauté for another 5 minutes, until the vegetables are soft and well browned.

2 Stir in the paprika, tomato paste, coconut milk, tomatoes, broth, and beans and bring to a boil. Reduce the heat and simmer, uncovered, for 12 minutes, until the vegetables are tender. Remove and discard the bay leaves

3 Stir in the cashew nuts and cilantro, season to taste with salt and black pepper, and heat through for 2 minutes. Serve with rice.

AFFORDABILITY 2

3 tablespoons vegetable oil
2 onions, chopped
2 small carrots, thinly sliced
3 garlic cloves, crushed
1 red bell pepper, cored, seeded, and chopped
2 bay leaves
1 tablespoon paprika
3 tablespoons tomato paste
1¾ cups coconut milk
¾ cup canned diced tomatoes
⅔ cup Vegetable Broth (see page 246)
1 (15 oz) can red kidney beans, rinsed and drained
1 cup unsalted, shelled cashew nuts, toasted
small handful of fresh cilantro, coarsely chopped
salt and black pepper
boiled black or white rice, to serve

Serves **4**
Prep time **10 minutes**
Cooking time **25 minutes**

OKRA & COCONUT STEW

V

12 oz okra
¼ cup vegetable oil
2 onions, chopped
2 green bell peppers, cored,
    seeded, and cut into chunks
3 celery sticks, thinly sliced
3 garlic cloves, crushed
4 teaspoons Cajun spice blend
½ teaspoon turmeric
1¼ cups Vegetable Broth
    (see page 246)
1¾ cups coconut milk
1⅓ cups frozen corn kernels
juice of 1 lime
¼ cup chopped fresh cilantro
salt and black pepper

Serves **3-4**
Prep time **15 minutes**
Cooking time **40 minutes**

1 Trim the stem ends from the okra and cut the pods into
¾ inch lengths.

2 Heat 2 tablespoons of the oil in a large saucepan and
sauté the okra for 5 minutes. Lift out with a slotted spoon
onto a plate.

3 Add the remaining oil to the pan and gently sauté the
onions, bell peppers, and celery for 10 minutes, stirring
frequently, until softened but not browned. Add the garlic,
spice blend, and turmeric and cook for 1 minute.

4 Pour in the broth and coconut milk and bring to a boil.
Reduce the heat, cover with a lid, and cook gently for
10 minutes. Return the okra to the pan with the corn kernels,
lime juice, and cilantro and cook for another 10 minutes. Season
to taste with salt and pepper and serve.

CHICKPEA & EGGPLANT STEW

1 Heat the oil in a large saucepan, add the onion and garlic, and cook over medium heat for 4-5 minutes, until softened. Stir in all the spices and cook, stirring, for 1 minute.

2 Add the eggplants and cook for about 5 minutes, until starting to soften. Stir in all the remaining ingredients, except the parsley, and season to taste with salt and black pepper.

3 Bring to a boil, then reduce the heat, cover with a lid, and simmer for 30 minutes, stirring occasionally. Stir in the parsley, then serve with couscous.

1 tablespoon vegetable oil
1 large onion, sliced
2 garlic cloves, crushed
1 teaspoon ground cumin
1 teaspoon ground cinnamon
1 teaspoon turmeric
1 teaspoon paprika
2 eggplants, chopped into 1½ inch chunks
2 carrots, sliced
1 cup dried pitted dates
1 (14½ oz) can diced tomatoes
1 (15 oz) can chickpeas, rinsed and drained
2½ cups Vegetable Broth (see page 246)
4 slices of preserved lemon (optional)
2 tablespoons chopped flat leaf parsley
salt and black pepper
couscous, to serve

Serves **4**
Prep time **10 minutes**
Cooking time **45 minutes**

COOKING TIP

Treat your freezer as your friend and cook double the amount so you can freeze half for another day. If you're taking the time to cook a stew, lasagne, chili, or casserole, it's a good idea to prepare more, then freeze it in single servings.

TOMATO & CHICKPEA STEW

V

1 Heat the oil in a large, heavy saucepan, add the onion, bell pepper, garlic, and ginger, and cook for 6-7 minutes, until softened.

2 Stir in the ground spices and cook for another minute. Add the tomato paste, broth, tomato wedges, and chickpeas, then cover with a lid and bring to a boil.

3 Season with salt and black pepper, reduce the heat, and simmer for about 8 minutes, until thickened slightly and the tomatoes have softened. Serve garnished with the chopped parsley.

2½ tablespoons vegetable oil
1 large onion, chopped
1 green bell pepper, cored, seeded, and chopped
1 garlic clove, chopped
1 inch piece of fresh ginger root, peeled and chopped
1 teaspoon ground cumin
1 teaspoon ground coriander
2 tablespoons tomato paste
2 cups Vegetable Broth (see page 246)
4 large tomatoes, each cut into 8 wedges
2 (15 oz) cans chickpeas, rinsed and drained
salt and black pepper
2 tablespoons chopped flat leaf parsley, to garnish

Serves **4**
Prep time **10 minutes**
Cooking time **20 minutes**

AFFORDABILITY

3 tablespoons vegetable oil
2 onions, coarsely chopped
2 carrots, sliced
2 parsnips, sliced
1 leek, trimmed and sliced
   into rings
1¾ cups dark beer or ale
2½ cups Vegetable Broth
   (see page 246)
½ cup pearl barley, rinsed
1 large potato, cut into
   ½ inch cubes
1 teaspoon dried thyme or
   mixed herbs
1-2 tablespoons grainy mustard
salt and black pepper

Dumplings
1¼ cups all-purpose flour
1¼ teaspoons baking powder
⅓ cup vegetable shortening

Serves **4-5**
Prep time **20 minutes**
Cooking time **1 hour**
20 minutes

BARLEY STEW

V

with Dumplings

1 Heat the oil in a large saucepan or flameproof casserole, add the onions, carrots, parsnips, and leeks and sauté gently for 10-15 minutes, stirring occasionally, until the vegetables are turning golden.

2 Add the beer and broth and bring to a boil. Reduce the heat to its lowest setting and add the barley, potato, thyme, and mustard. Cover with a lid and cook gently for about 40 minutes, stirring occasionally, until thickened and the barley is just tender. If the stew dries out a little, add a little water because the dumplings will absorb some of the liquid as they cook. Season to taste with salt and black pepper.

3 Make the dumplings. Put the flour, baking powder, shortening, and a little salt and black pepper into a bowl. Add ⅔ cup cold water and stir with a blunt knife to make a soft dough.

4 Take tablespoons of the dough and spoon over the stew. Replace the lid and cook for another 20 minutes, until the dumplings are light and fluffy.

Goulash with CHIVE DUMPLINGS

V

¼ cup vegetable oil
8 pearl onions, peeled
2 garlic cloves, crushed
1 carrot, chopped
1 large celery stick, sliced
4 potatoes, cubed
1 teaspoon caraway seeds
1 teaspoon smoked paprika
1 (14½ oz) can diced tomatoes
2 cups Vegetable Broth
  (see page 246)
salt and black pepper

Chive dumplings
⅔ cup all-purpose flour
½ teaspoon baking powder
½ teaspoon salt
¼ cup vegetable shortening
1 tablespoon chopped chives

Serves **4**
Prep time **20 minutes**
Cooking time **50 minutes**

1 Heat the oil in a large saucepan, add the onions, garlic, carrot, celery, potatoes, and caraway seeds, and cook over medium heat for 10 minutes, stirring frequently. Add the paprika and cook, stirring, for 1 minute.

2 Stir in the tomatoes, broth, and salt and black pepper to taste. Bring to a boil, then reduce the heat, cover with a lid, and simmer gently for 20 minutes.

3 Make the dumplings. Sift the flour, baking powder, and salt into a bowl and stir in the shortening, chives, and black pepper to taste. Working quickly and lightly, gradually mix in 4–5 tablespoons water to form a soft dough. Divide into eight equal pieces and roll into balls.

4 Carefully arrange the dumplings in the stew, leaving gaps between them, replace the lid, and simmer for 15 minutes, until doubled in size and light and fluffy.

AFFORDABILITY **1**

Lentil & Parsnip CASSEROLE

1 tablespoon vegetable oil
1 large onion, chopped
2 celery sticks, finely sliced
4 carrots, chopped
4 cups chopped
  cremini mushrooms
2 (15 oz) cans green lentils in
  water, rinsed and drained, or
  4 cups cooked green lentils
1 (14½ oz) can diced tomatoes
1 tablespoon tomato paste
1¼ cups Vegetable Broth
  (see page 246)
2 teaspoons dried mixed herbs
4 parsnips, peeled and chopped
4 russet or Yukon gold
  potatoes, peeled and chopped
2 tablespoons milk
2 tablespoons butter
½ cup shredded sharp cheddar
  or American cheese
salt and black pepper

1 Heat the oil in a large saucepan, add the onion, celery, and carrots, and cook for 3-4 minutes, until softened. Increase the heat, stir in the mushrooms, and cook for another 3 minutes, stirring occasionally.

2 Add the lentils, tomatoes, tomato paste, broth, and dried herbs. Bring to a boil, then reduce the heat and simmer, uncovered, for 15 minutes. Season to taste with salt and black pepper. Transfer to a 2 quart ovenproof dish.

3 Meanwhile, cook the parsnips and potatoes in a large saucepan of lightly salted boiling water for 20 minutes or until tender. Drain the root vegetables and return to the pan. Mash with the milk and butter, then season to taste with salt and black pepper.

4 Spoon the mashed parsnip and potatoes over the lentil mixture and sprinkle with the cheese. Bake in a preheated oven, at 375°F, for 20 minutes, until golden and bubbling.

Serves **6**
Prep time **20 minutes**
Cooking time **45 minutes**

Lentil & Tomato CHUNKY STEW

1 Finely chop the onion, carrot, celery, and garlic. (You can do this in a food processor or blender, if you have one.)

2 Heat the oil in a large, heavy casserole or saucepan, add the vegetable mixture, and cook for 5-6 minutes, stirring frequently, until softened and lightly golden.

3 Pour in the red wine or grape juice, ½ cup water, the tomato paste, diced tomatoes, and herbs, then season to taste with salt and black pepper. Bring to a boil, then reduce the heat and simmer gently for about 15 minutes.

4 Add the lentils and simmer for another 5-7 minutes, until thickened and tender. Spoon into warm deep bowls, sprinkle with cheese, and serve with plenty of fresh, crusty bread.

AFFORDABILITY 1

1 onion, coarsely chopped
1 carrot, coarsely chopped
1 celery stick, coarsely chopped
1 garlic clove, peeled
3 tablespoons vegetable oil
½ cup red wine, or red grape juice
¼ cup tomato paste
1 (14½ oz) can diced tomatoes
1 teaspoon dried mixed herbs
2 (15 oz) cans green lentils, rinsed and drained, or 4 cups cooked green lentils
salt and black pepper

To serve
½ cup grated vegetarian Parmesan-style cheese
crusty bread

Serves **4**
Prep time **10 minutes**
Cooking time **25-30 minutes**

Creative LEFTOVERS

The word "leftovers" doesn't exactly conjure up images of culinary delights, but when you're eating on a budget, you need to make sure you use all the food you buy and come up with smart ways to liven up leftovers. You probably wouldn't think twice about zapping the remains of last night's pizza in the microwave for a midmorning snack, so there's no excuse for throwing away perfectly good vegetables, fruit, or pasta simply because you cooked too much.

KEEP IT COOL

If you're keeping food to use the next day, it's important to let it cool, then cover it and keep it in the refrigerator so it stays fresh. Don't worry if you only have a small amount of one or two ingredients—you can combine them to make a whole dish, or add them to an existing recipe. It's best to use leftovers the following day. If you happen to find something lurking in a bowl in the back of the refrigerator, always check with your housemates how long it's been there—economizing is great but not at the risk of food poisoning.

SLICE IT UP

Leftovers are ideal for soups, stews, and casseroles. With a good selection of spices, vegetable bouillon cubes, and sauces in the cupboards and a ready supply of canned diced tomatoes, the key is to think of a dish that includes the ingredients you have instead of just reheating your leftovers and piling them onto a plate. There are a few ideas below to give you some inspiration.

QUICK FIXES FOR LEFTOVERS

- Make potato cakes with leftover mashed potatoes.
- Slice leftover roasted potatoes to make a potato casserole or scalloped potatoes.
- Mix cold cooked pasta with a spoon of pesto or mayonnaise for a pasta salad.
- Most vegetables can be pureed to make a soup or chopped for a spicy casserole.
- Use leftover rice to make a jambalaya or fried rice dish.
- Use leftover vegetables and pasta to make a pasta casserole or gratin—top with grated cheese and bread crumbs.
- Slightly overripe bananas are perfect for banana bread or muffins.
- Any combination of green beans, asparagus, broccoli, potato, and bell peppers can be used to make a frittata.
- If your loaf of bread has seen better days, try a bread and butter pudding— cheap, easy, and delicious
- Chop leftover vegetables and add to steamed couscous.

BUTTERED CAULIFLOWER GRATIN

1 Cut the cauliflower into large florets and blanch in a saucepan boiling water for 2 minutes. Drain thoroughly.

2 Melt half of the butter in a large skillet. Add the bread crumbs and sauté for 2 minutes, until golden. Drain and set aside.

3 Melt the remaining butter in the pan with the oil. Add the cauliflower florets and sauté gently for about 5 minutes, until golden. Add the capers, pickles, dill or tarragon, and sour cream, season to taste with salt and black pepper, and stir over medium heat for 1 minute.

4 Turn into a shallow flameproof dish and sprinkle with the fried bread crumbs and grated cheese. Cook under a preheated medium broiler for about 2 minutes, until the crumbs are dark golden brown.

1 large cauliflower
2 tablespoons butter
1 cup fresh bread crumbs
2 tablespoons olive oil
3 tablespoons capers, drained
3 baby dill pickles, finely chopped
3 tablespoons chopped dill or tarragon
½ cup sour cream
¼ cup grated vegetarian Parmesan-style cheese
salt and black pepper

Serves 4
Prep time 10 minutes
Cooking time 15 minutes

CAULIFLOWER
& Cheese

1 If using baby cauliflowers, trim the bottom of each to flatten. Lightly grease a shallow flameproof dish.

2 Make the sauce. Melt the butter in a heavy saucepan. Gently heat the milk in a separate saucepan. Stir the flour into the melted butter and cook over low heat for 2-3 minutes, stirring occasionally. Remove the pan from the heat and pour in a little of the warm milk, stirring constantly. Gradually add the rest of the milk, again stirring constantly. Add the bay leaves and nutmeg and season well. Return the pan to a low heat and cook for 10-12 minutes (or until there is no taste of flour), stirring frequently. Remove and discard the bay leaves. Stir in the cheddar and remove from the heat.

3 Meanwhile, cook the cauliflower in a saucepan of boiling water for 5-6 minutes. Drain well, then place in the dish and pour over the sauce.

4 Sprinkle with the Parmesan-style cheese and cook under a preheated medium-high broiler for 1 minute, until lightly browned. Serve immediately.

8 baby cauliflowers or
  1 large cauliflower, cut
  into large florets
3 tablespoons butter,
  plus extra for greasing
2 cups milk
⅓ cup all-purpose flour
2 bay leaves
pinch of grated nutmeg
3 cups shredded sharp
  cheddar or American cheese
¼ cup grated vegetarian
  Parmesan-style cheese
salt and black pepper

Serves 4
Prep time 10 minutes
Cooking time 20-25 minutes

BEAN CASSEROLE

AFFORDABILITY
1

1½ lb small new potatoes
3 tablespoons vegetable oil
1 onion, chopped
1 celery stick, chopped
2 garlic cloves, chopped
3 tablespoons homemade
  (see page 249) or store-
  bought pesto
4 ripe tomatoes, diced
¼ pint hot Vegetable Broth
  (see page 246) or water
1 (15 oz) can cranberry, navy,
  or pinto beans, rinsed and
  drained
1 cup fresh or frozen green
  beans, thawed if frozen
  (1 inch pieces)
½ cup grated vegetarian
  Parmesan-style cheese
salt and black pepper

Serves **4**
Prep time **15 minutes**
Cooking time **20 minutes**

1 Cook the new potatoes in a saucepan of lightly salted boiling water for about 10 minutes, until just tender. Drain and cool slightly, then cut into ¼ inch slices.

2 Meanwhile, heat 2 tablespoons of the oil in a large skillet, add the onion, and cook for 2 minutes. Add the celery and cook for another 2 minutes, then add the garlic and continue to cook for 2-3 minutes, stirring frequently, until lightly golden.

3 Stir the pesto into the onions, then add the diced tomatoes, broth or water, cranberry, navy, or pinto beans, and green beans. Season generously with salt and black pepper and bring to a boil, then reduce the heat and simmer for 5 minutes, until the tomatoes soften and the beans are tender.

4 Transfer the vegetable mixture to a large flameproof dish and arrange the sliced potatoes over the top. Sprinkle with the grated cheese, drizzle with the remaining oil, and cook under a preheated broiler for 7-8 minutes, until golden.

GNOCCHI
WITH SAGE BUTTER

1 Cook the potatoes in a saucepan of lightly salted boiling water for 10–12 minutes, until tender. Drain, return the potatoes to the pan, and heat gently for several seconds to dry out.

2 Mash the potatoes and beat in the egg, salt, oil, and flour to form a sticky dough. Take walnut-size pieces of the dough and roll into egg shapes, rolling them over the tines of a fork.

3 Bring a large saucepan of lightly salted water to a rolling boil, add half the gnocchi (freeze the remainder for later use), and cook for 3 minutes, until they rise to the surface. Drain the gnocchi and transfer to serving bowls.

4 Meanwhile, melt the butter in a skillet. As soon as it stops foaming, add the sage and sauté over medium-high heat, stirring, for 2–3 minutes, until crisp and the butter turns golden brown. Drizzle the butter over the gnocchi, sprinkle with grated cheese, and serve immediately.

4 russet or Yukon gold potatoes, cubed
1 egg, beaten
1 teaspoon sea salt
2 tablespoons olive oil
1⅓ cups all-purpose flour
1 stick butter
2 tablespoons chopped sage
salt
grated vegetarian Parmesan-style cheese, to serve

Serves 4
Prep time **30 minutes**
Cooking time **20 minutes**

POTATO & ONION PIZZA

AFFORDABILITY 1

3 tablespoons olive oil, plus extra for greasing
2⅓ cups all-purpose flour
2¼ teaspoons or 1 (¼ oz) envelope active dry yeast
1½ teaspoons sugar
1 teaspoon salt
½ cup sour cream
8 oz unpeeled new potatoes, thinly sliced
½ onion, thinly sliced
2 teaspoons dried thyme
1 cup shredded Swiss, American, or mozzarella cheese
12 pitted black ripe olives (optional)
black pepper

Serves **4**
Prep time **20 minutes**
Cooking time **20 minutes**

1 Lightly oil a baking sheet. In a large bowl, mix together the flour, yeast, sugar, and salt. Make a well in the center and pour in ¾ cup warm water and 2 tablespoons of the oil. Combine to make a soft dough, then roll out to a rectangle about 14 x 10 inches. Transfer to the baking sheet and bake in a preheated oven, at 400°F, for 5 minutes or until just beginning to brown.

2 Spoon ¼ cup of the sour cream over the pizza crust. Top with the slices of potato and onion, then sprinkle with the thyme and cheese. Drizzle the remaining oil over the pizza and return to the oven. Increase the temperature to 425°F and bake for about 15 minutes, until golden.

3 Cut the pizza into slices, sprinkle with the olives, if using, and top with the remaining sour cream. Season with black pepper and serve hot.

Roasted &Baked

BEAN & POTATO MOUSSAKA

CHEESE & TOMATO MUFFINS
WITH BASIL

QUICK MEDITERRANEAN FOCACCIA

Stuffed RED ONIONS

4 large red onions, peeled
2 tablespoons olive oil
2 cups finely chopped
 white mushrooms
½ cup bulgur wheat
1 tablespoon chopped parsley
1 tablespoon golden raisins
1 tablespoon grated vegetarian
 Parmesan-style cheese
 (optional)
salt and black pepper

Serves 4
Prep time **30 minutes**
Cooking time **1 ½ hours**

1 Cut the top off each onion and scoop out the centers, using a teaspoon. Heat the oil in a skillet. Finely chop the scooped-out onion, then add to the pan and sauté until soft and golden brown. Add the mushrooms and cook, stirring, for another 5 minutes.

2 Meanwhile, bring a large saucepan of water to a boil. Add the onion cups and simmer for 10 minutes or until they begin to soften. Drain well.

3 Add the bulgar, parsley, salt, black pepper, and 1¼ cups water to the mushrooms. Boil for 5 minutes. Cover the pan, and simmer for another 30 minutes or until the grains have softened. Add extra water if needed.

4 Stir the golden raisins into the bulgur mixture and spoon into the onions. Put the onions in a roasting pan and cover with aluminum foil. Cook in a preheated oven, at 375°F, for 30 minutes. Remove the foil, sprinkle with the cheese, if using, and cook for another 10 minutes.

AFFORDABILITY
1

FETA-STUFFED PEPPERS

1 Cook the bulgur wheat in 2½ cups of the broth in a covered saucepan for 10 minutes.

2 Lay each bell pepper on a cutting board and make a cut from the bottom up toward and around the stem, opening out enough to remove the core and seeds but not so much that the bell pepper splits in two.

3 Drain off any excess broth from the cooked bulgur, add the golden raisins, allspice, feta, a little of the basil, and some salt and black pepper. Mix together and spoon into the prepared bell peppers. Transfer to a roasting pan.

4 Heat 1 tablespoon of the oil in a skillet, add the onion, and sauté for 5 minutes, until lightly browned. Add the garlic, tomatoes, remaining broth, and a little salt and black pepper. Spoon around the bell peppers and sprinkle with a little more torn basil.

5 Drizzle the bell peppers with the remaining oil and cook in a preheated oven, at 400°F, for 30 minutes or until the bell peppers are soft. Serve garnished with the remaining basil.

1 cup bulgur wheat
3⅓ cups Vegetable Broth (see page 246)
2 orange bell peppers
2 yellow bell peppers
¼ cup golden raisins
¼ teaspoon ground allspice
⅔ cup crumbled feta cheese
1 small bunch of basil, torn
3 tablespoons olive oil
1 onion, chopped
3 garlic cloves, finely chopped
4 tomatoes, coarsely chopped
salt and black pepper

Serves 4
Prep time 20 minutes
Cooking time 45 minutes

AFFORDABILITY
2

Baked Peppers
WITH GOAT CHEESE

4 red bell peppers, halved, cored, and seeded
1 (15 oz) can great Northern beans, rinsed and drained
4 teaspoons olive oil
4 oz firm goat cheese
8 teaspoons homemade (see page 249) or store-bought pesto

Serves **4**
Prep time **5 minutes**
Cooking time **30 minutes**

1 Put the bell pepper halves on a baking sheet, skin side down, and divide the great Northen beans among them. Drizzle with the oil.

2 Cut the goat cheese horizontally into 2 slices and arrange them on top of the bell peppers. Top each one with 1 teaspoon pesto.

3 Cover the bell peppers with aluminum foil and bake in a preheated oven, at 400°F, for 20 minutes or until the bell peppers are tender. Remove the foil and bake for another 10 minutes.

AFFORDABILITY 2

BROCCOLI & SPINACH EGGAHS

vegetable oil, for greasing
¼ broccoli
3½ cups baby spinach
6 eggs
1¼ cups low-fat milk
2 tablespoons grated
   vegetarian Parmesan-style
   cheese
large pinch of ground nutmeg
salt and black pepper

Makes **12**
Prep time **15 minutes**
Cooking time **20 minutes**

1 Lightly oil the holes of a deep 12-cup muffin pan. Cut the broccoli into small florets and thickly slice the stems. Put into a steamer set over boiling water, cover with a lid, and cook for 3 minutes. Add the spinach and cook for another 1 minute or until the spinach has just wilted.

2 Beat the eggs, milk, cheese, nutmeg, and a little salt and black pepper together in a small bowl.

3 Divide the broccoli and spinach among the prepare cups of the muffin pan and cover with the egg mixture. Bake in a preheated oven, at 375°F, for about 15 minutes or until lightly browned, well risen, and the egg mixture has set. Let rest in the pan for 1-2 minutes, then loosen the edges with a knife and turn out.

AFFORDABILITY
1

BROCCOLI & BLUE CHEESE SOUFFLÉS

1 Brush four 1¼ cup ramekins with melted butter and sprinkle with bread crumbs to coat the bottom and sides.

2 Blanch the broccoli in a saucepan of boiling water until almost tender, then blend with an immersion blender, or a food processor or blender if you have one, until smooth.

3 Melt the butter in a saucepan, add the flour, and cook for 2 minutes. Gradually add the milk, stirring constantly, and bring to a boil. Boil for 2 minutes, until thick. Remove from the heat and stir in the spices and egg yolks. Season well and stir in the pureed broccoli and cheese.

4 In a clean bowl, whisk the egg whites until stiff. Using a metal spoon, carefully fold the egg whites into the broccoli and cheese mixture.

5 Pour into the ramekins, almost up to the rim. Run your finger around the inside edge of the ramekins to help the soufflés rise straight up. Bake on a preheated hot baking sheet in a preheated oven, at 400°F, for 8-10 minutes or until risen. Serve immediately.

4 tablespoons butter, plus extra melted butter for greasing
handful of fine fresh white bread crumbs
3 cups broccoli florets
⅓ cup all-purpose flour
1¼ cups milk
1 teaspoon smoked paprika
pinch of grated nutmeg
4 extra-large eggs, separated
⅔ cup crumbled creamy blue cheese
salt and black pepper

Serves 4
Prep time **20 minutes**
Cooking time **15 minutes**

AFFORDABILITY
1

Butternut & Egglant Tikka

1 small butternut squash
  (about 1 lb), peeled, seeded,
  and cut into 1 inch cubes
1 small eggplant, cut into
  1 inch cubes
6 shallots, quartered
3 tablespoons vegetable oil
2 garlic cloves, finely chopped
¼ cup tikka masala curry paste
  (suitable for vegetarians)
¾ cup canned diced tomatoes
1 tablespoon mango chutney
salt
3 tablespoons plain yogurt
chopped fresh cilantro,
  to garnish
warmed naan or boiled basmati
  or other long-grain rice,
  to serve

Serves **2**
Prep time **20 minutes**
Cooking time **1 hour 5 minutes**

1 Spread out the squash in a roasting pan or shallow baking dish with the eggplant and shallots. Drizzle with the oil and bake in a preheated oven, at 400°F, for about 50 minutes, turning the ingredients once or twice, until golden and almost tender.

2 Mix the garlic with the curry paste, tomatoes, chutney, and a little salt and spoon into the dish, stirring the vegetables to coat in the sauce.

3 Return to the oven and cook for another 10 minutes. Stir in the yogurt and continue to cook for 5 minutes, until hot and bubbling.

4 Sprinkle with cilantro and serve with naan or rice.

Bean & Potato MOUSSAKA

1 Cook the potatoes in a large saucepan of boiling water for about 10 minutes, until just tender. Drain and let rest until cool enough to handle, then remove the skins and slice into ¼ inch slices.

2 Heat the oil in a large saucepan, add the onion and garlic, and sauté gently for 3-4 minutes, until softened. Add the carrot, cinnamon, and herbs, then stir in the tomatoes, kidney beans, and broth. Season to taste with salt and black pepper and bring to a boil, then reduce the heat and simmer, uncovered, for 15 minutes, until thickened.

3 Meanwhile, make the sauce. Put the butter, flour, and milk into a saucepan and whisk constantly over medium heat until the sauce boils and thickens. Simmer for 2-3 minutes, until you have a smooth, glossy sauce. Stir in the cheese and then remove from the heat. Let cool slightly, then beat in the egg.

4 Put half the bean mixture into the bottom of a deep ovenproof dish and top with a layer of the potatoes. Repeat, finishing with a layer of potatoes. Pour the sauce over the potatoes and bake in a preheated oven, at 350°F, for 25-30 minutes, until golden brown. Let stand for 5 minutes before serving.

6 red-skinned or white round
  potatoes (about 1½ lb),
  washed
1 tablespoon vegetable oil
1 large onion, chopped
1 garlic clove, crushed
1 large carrot, sliced
1 teaspoon ground cinnamon
2 teaspoons dried mixed herbs
1 (14½ oz) can diced tomatoes
1 (15 oz) can red kidney beans,
  rinsed and drained
1¼ cups Vegetable Broth
  (see page 246)
4 tablespoons butter
⅓ cup all-purpose flour
2½ cups milk
¾ cup shredded cheddar or
  Monterey Jack cheese
1 egg
salt and black pepper

Serves **4**
Prep time **15 minutes,
 plus cooling**
Cooking time **55-60 minutes**

AFFORDABILITY
1

Melanzane PARMIGIANA

6 eggplants
2 tablespoons olive oil
2 (14½ oz) cans diced tomatoes
2 garlic cloves, crushed
2 cups shredded cheddar or
   mozzarella cheese
½ cup grated vegetarian
   Parmesan-style cheese
salt and black pepper

Serves **6**
Prep time **15 minutes**
Cooking time **50 minutes**

1 Trim the eggplants and cut lengthwise into thick slices. Brush them with half the oil and place on two large baking sheets. Roast at the top of a preheated oven, at 400°F, for 10 minutes on each side, until golden and tender.

2 Meanwhile, put the tomatoes and garlic into a saucepan and bring to a boil. Reduce the heat and simmer for 10 minutes, then season with salt and black pepper.

3 Spoon a little of the tomato into an ovenproof dish and top with a layer of eggplants and some of the cheddar or mozzarella. Continue with the layers, finishing with a layer of cheddar on top. Sprinkle with the Parmesan-style cheese and bake for 30 minutes, until the cheese is bubbling and golden.

AFFORDABILITY
2

CHUNKY PEANUT LOG
with Homemade Coleslaw

1 Heat the oil in a saucepan, add the onions, and sauté for 5 minutes, until softened. Transfer to a bowl and add the spices, peanuts, bread crumbs, and cilantro. Mix well. Add the eggs to the bowl and stir well until combined.

2 Brush a large square of aluminum foil with oil. Turn out the peanut mixture onto the foil and shape into a log about 7 inches long. Roll the foil up around the log and twist the ends to resemble a wrapped candy. Bake in a preheated oven, at 350°F, for 25 minutes.

3 Meanwhile, put the cabbage, shallot, and parsley into a bowl. Quarter, core, and thinly slice the apples and add to the bowl. Mix together the mayonnaise, yogurt, and celery seeds or celery salt, if using, with a little black pepper and add to the bowl. Mix well.

4 Serve the peanut log thickly sliced with the coleslaw.

AFFORDABILITY 1

2 tablespoons vegetable oil, plus extra for greasing
2 red onions, chopped
2 teaspoons paprika
1 teaspoon ground cumin
1 cup salted peanuts
2/3 cup roasted, unsalted peanuts
1 cup fresh whole wheat or white bread crumbs
1/3 cup chopped fresh cilantro
2 eggs, beaten
black pepper

Coleslaw
1/2 small green cabbage, shredded
1 shallot, chopped
3 tablespoons chopped parsley
2 red crisp, sweet apples
1/3 cup mayonnaise
1/3 cup plain yogurt
1/4 teaspoon celery seeds or celery salt (optional)

Serves **4**
Prep time **25 minutes**
Cooking time **30 minutes**

RED ONION & Gruyère POPOVERS

3 red onions (about 1¼ lb), quartered
1 tablespoon coarsely chopped rosemary
¼ cup vegetable oil
1 cup all-purpose flour
2 eggs
1¼ cups milk
1⅓ cups shredded Gruyère or Swiss cheese
salt and black pepper
green vegetable or baked beans, to serve

Serves 4
Prep time **20 minutes**
Cooking time **1 hour**

1 Spread out the onions and rosemary in a shallow roasting pan and drizzle with 2 tablespoons of the oil. Mix well and cook in a preheated oven, at 400°F, for 30 minutes, until the onions are soft and lightly browned.

2 Meanwhile, put the flour into a bowl and make a well in the center. Break the eggs into the well with a little of the milk. Whisk the eggs and milk together, gradually working in the flour to make a thick paste. Once the paste is smooth, gradually beat in the remaining milk, a little salt, plenty of black pepper, and one-third of the cheese.

3 Pour the remaining oil around the onions and return to the oven for 5 minutes to get the oil really hot. Pour the batter around the onions and sprinkle with the remaining cheese. Return to the oven for 25-30 minutes, until well risen and golden. Serve with green vegetables or baked beans.

AFFORDABILITY
1

TRICOLORE
CAULIFLOWER GRATIN

AFFORDABILITY

1

3 tomatoes, sliced
7 cups trimmed spinach
pinch of grated nutmeg
1 cauliflower, cut into florets
3 tablespoons butter
⅓ cup all-purpose flour
2 cups low-fat milk
1½ cups shredded sharp
   cheddar, Swiss, or
   American cheese
½ slice of bread, torn into
   tiny pieces
2 tablespoons sunflower seeds
2 tablespoons pumpkin seeds
salt and black pepper

Serves **4**
Prep time **15 minutes**
Cooking time **30 minutes**

1 Arrange the tomatoes in the bottom of a shallow ovenproof dish. Steam the spinach for 1-2 minutes, until just wilted, then spoon them over the tomatoes. Sprinkle with a little nutmeg and some salt and black pepper. Steam the cauliflower for 8-10 minutes, until just tender.

2 Meanwhile, melt the butter in a separate saucepan and stir in the flour. Gradually whisk in the milk and bring to a boil, stirring constantly, until smooth and thick. Stir in two-thirds of the cheese and season well.

3 Arrange the cauliflower on top of the spinach, then gently mix together. Pour the sauce over the top. Mix the remaining cheese with the torn bread and seeds, then sprinkle over the cheese sauce.

4 Bake in a preheated oven, at 400°F, for 20 minutes, until the topping is crisp and golden and the vegetables are piping hot.

SPINACH & POTATO GRATIN

AFFORDABILITY 2

butter, for greasing
5 red-skinned or white round
    potatoes (about 1¼ lb),
    peeled and thinly sliced
1 lb spinach, trimmed
2 cups shredded mozzarella
    cheese
4 tomatoes, sliced
3 eggs, beaten
1¼ cups heavy cream
salt and black pepper

Serves 4
Prep time **15 minutes**
Cooking time **35 minutes**

1 Grease a large ovenproof dish. Cook the potatoes in a large saucepan of salted boiling water for 5 minutes, then drain well.

2 Meanwhile, cook the spinach in a separate saucepan of boiling water for 1-2 minutes. Drain and squeeze out the excess water.

3 Line the bottom of the prepared dish with half the potato slices. Cover with the spinach and half the mozzarella, seasoning each layer well with salt and black pepper. Cover with the remaining potato slices and arrange the tomato slices on top. Sprinkle with the remaining mozzarella.

4 Beat the eggs and cream together in a bowl and season well with salt and black pepper. Pour the sauce over the ingredients in the dish. Bake in a preheated oven, at 350°F, for about 30 minutes. Serve immediately.

LIMA BEAN & VEGETABLE NUT CASSEROLE

1⅓ cups all-purpose flour
6 tablespoons cold butter, diced
1 cup chopped walnuts
½ cup shredded cheddar or
   mozzarella cheese
1 (16 oz) package prepared
   broccoli, cauliflower, and
   carrots, thawed if frozen
2 cups prepared tomato and
   herb sauce
2 garlic cloves, crushed
⅓ cup finely chopped basil
1 (15 oz) can lima beans, rinsed
   and drained
salt and black pepper

Serves **4**
Prep time **15 minutes**
Cooking time **20-25 minutes**

1 To make a crumb topping, put the flour into a bowl, add the butter, and rub in with the fingertips until the mixture resembles bread crumbs. Stir in the chopped walnuts and shredded cheese, season, and set aside.

2 Remove the carrots from the prepared vegetables, coarsely chop, and boil for 2 minutes. Add the broccoli and cauliflower and cook for another minute, then drain.

3 Meanwhile, heat the tomato and herb sauce in a large saucepan until bubbling. Stir in the garlic, basil, lima beans, and blanched vegetables.

4 Transfer the bean mixture to a medium ovenproof dish and sprinkle the crumb topping over it. Bake in a preheated oven, at 400°F, for 15-20 minutes or until golden and bubbling.

AFFORDABILITY 2

STUDENT TIP

Look for discount coupons in your local papers and take advantage of online shopping deals from the big retailers. Many have introductory offers for new customers—but that doesn't mean you have to continue shopping with them once you've taken advantage of the deals.

Dinner Dates
WITH PALS

Although much of your socializing will involve the odd package of potato chips or some fries washed down with a cool drink or coffee, you might occasionally want to leave the gloomy interior of a fast food outlet and host a gathering at home. The days of formal dinner parties are long gone, which ties in nicely with the less salubrious nature of student life, and you don't need to be a gourmet chef to put together a decent meal. Nobody will expect Michelin Stars to light up the dining table. In fact, many of your friends will be so grateful for a free meal that any culinary catastrophes will be totally overlooked.

MISMATCH CHIC

These days, trendy hosts are leaving their expensive dinner plates gathering dust in the attic and are instead laying the table with an eclectic mix of plates, cutlery, and decorations. As a student, you probably won't have much choice in the matter and, depending on numbers, you might have to borrow extra knives, forks, and plates for your dinner party. A few flowers in a cleaned-out jar or two or mismatched candles will complete the shabby-chic look and you can hold your head up high as a trendsetter.

LOVE THE LIST

If shopping tends to involve ad hoc visits to the convenience store, you'll need to be more organized if you're inviting people around for dinner. Start by choosing your menu. Forget the three-course affair followed by coffee and cheese served in an exclusive restaurant; you're looking for low-maintenance meals that you can ideally prep in advance. That way, you can do all the sweating, swearing, and kitchen full of smoke well before your pals arrive and be the perfect stress-free host or hostess at dinnertime. If you want to make an appetizer, choose something that can be plated up ahead of time and served cold. Likewise, pick a dessert that's easy to dish out after a few glasses of wine, or buy some ice cream.

Write a list of all the ingredients you need and go to a large supermarket to make sure you can get everything in one shopping trip. If you're shopping a day or two ahead of your gathering, make sure you check the expiration dates so you don't end up with a key ingredient going to waste. If you share cupboard or refrigerator space with your housemates, let them know that your recent purchases are strictly out of bounds for late-night raids.

CONVERTING THE CARNIVORES

Don't forget that you might be inviting hardened carnivores to your dining table. Treat them gently by keeping your menu simple and recognizable. It might be doing them a disservice to say they'll turn their noses up at quinoa or bean sprouts, but meat lovers can be a little less adventurous when it comes to veggie food. The idea is to showcase meat-free meals, not put people off.

ROOT VEGETABLE & BEAN GRATIN

AFFORDABILITY
1

1 Heat the oil in a large saucepan, add the carrots, parsnips, and leeks, and cook over medium heat for 4-5 minutes, until slightly softened.

2 Stir the wine or grape juice into the pan and cook until reduced by half, then stir in the tomatoes, broth, beans, and rosemary. Season well with salt and black pepper, then cover with a lid and simmer for 15 minutes, stirring occasionally. Transfer to a 2 quart ovenproof dish.

3 Meanwhile, make the crumb topping. Put the bread, walnuts, parsley, and ¾ cup of the cheese into a food processor or blender and pulse until the mixture resembles bread crumbs. Alternatively, blend the ingredients, in batches, using an immersion blender.

4 Spoon the topping over the vegetable mixture and sprinkle the remaining cheese over the top. Bake in a preheated oven, at 350°F, for 25-30 minutes, until golden and crisp.

1 tablespoon olive oil
2 carrots, sliced
2 parsnips, peeled and chopped
2 leeks, trimmed and sliced
1¼ cups red wine or red grape juice
1 (14½ oz) can diced tomatoes
1¼ cups Vegetable Broth (see page 246)
1 (14 oz) can lima or cannellini (white kidney) beans, rinsed and drained
1 tablespoon chopped rosemary
salt and black pepper

Crumb topping
3½ slices whol wheat bread, coarsely torn into pieces
½ cup coarsely chopped walnuts
2 tablespoons chopped flat leaf parsley
1 cup shredded cheddar, American, or Monterey Jack cheese

Serves 4-6
Prep time 20 minutes
Cooking time 50-55 minutes

LENTIL & CABBAGE CASSEROLE

THE POTATOES AND CABBAGE IN THIS RECIPE ARE COOKED IN A STEAMER, WHICH RETAINS MORE NUTRIENTS THAN BOILING. IF YOU DON'T HAVE A STEAMER, BOIL THE VEGETABLES IN AS LITTLE WATER AS POSSIBLE AND ADD THEM ONLY WHEN THE WATER IS PIPING HOT.

1 tablespoon vegetable oil
1 onion, finely chopped
8 carrots (about 1 lb), diced
2 garlic cloves, finely chopped
1 (15 oz) can low-sugar,
  low-sodium baked beans
²/₃ cup dried red lentils
2 cups Vegetable Broth
  (see page 246)
salt and black pepper

Topping
6 russet (about 1½ lb)
2 cups finely shredded
  savoy cabbage
3–4 tablespoons low-fat milk
1 cup shredded cheddar or
  American cheese

Serves 4
Prep time **30 minutes**
Cooking time **35 minutes**

1 Heat the oil in a saucepan, add the onion, and sauté for about 5 minutes, stirring occasionally, until softened. Stir in the carrots and garlic and sauté for 2 minutes.

2 Mix in the baked beans, lentils, and broth and season to taste. Bring to a boil, then reduce the heat, cover with a lid, and simmer for 20 minutes, until the lentils are tender, adding extra liquid, if necessary.

3 Meanwhile, make the topping. Cut the potatoes into large chunks and cook them in the bottom of a steamer filled halfway with boiling water for 15 minutes. Add the steamer top, fill with the cabbage, cover with a lid, and cook for 5 minutes, until both cabbage and potatoes are tender.

4 Drain the potatoes, return them to the pan, and mash with the milk. Stir in the cabbage and two-thirds of the cheese.

5 Spoon the hot carrot mixture into the bottom of a 1½ quart flameproof pie plate. Spoon the potato mixture on top, then sprinkle with the remaining cheese. Place under a preheated hot broiler for 5 minutes, until golden brown.

AFFORDABILITY 1

MOROCCAN-STYLE
SWEET POTATO
Pie

2 tablespoons vegetable oil
1 large onion, coarsely chopped
1 large fennel bulb, coarsely
  chopped
1 tablespoon ras el hanout
  Moroccan spice blend
2 garlic cloves, chopped
2 teaspoons all-purpose flour
4-5 sweet potatoes (about
  1½ lb), scrubbed and cut into
  ¾ inch chunks
2 cups Vegetable Broth
  (see page 246)
⅓ cup coarsely chopped,
  dried pitted dates
3 tablespoons chopped mint
1 (1 lb) package puff pastry
  (thawed if frozen)
flour, for dusting
beaten egg, or milk, to glaze
salt and black pepper

Serves **4**
Prep time **25 minutes,
plus cooling**
Cooking time **1 hour**

1 Heat the oil in a saucepan or large skillet, add the onion and
fennel, and gently sauté for 5 minutes, until softened. Stir in
the spice blend, garlic, and flour and cook for another 1 minute.

2 Add the sweet potatoes and broth and bring to a boil.
Reduce the heat to its lowest setting, cover with a lid,
and cook gently for 15 minutes. Stir in the dates and mint,
season to taste with salt and black pepper, and let cool.

3 Turn the mixture into a pie plate. Roll out the pastry on
a lightly floured surface until large enough to cover the
pie plate. Brush the edges of the pie plate with water and lift
the lid into position, pressing the pastry firmly around the rim.
Trim off the excess pastry and make a hole in the center of the
pie for the steam to escape.

4 Brush the top of the pastry with beaten egg or milk and
bake in a preheated oven, at 400°F, for 35 minutes, until
the pastry is risen and deep golden.

MOZZARELLA
PHYLLO PACKAGES

UNFORTUNATELY, PHYLLO PASTRY SHEETS VARY CONSIDERABLY IN SIZE, SO KEEP THIS IN MIND WHEN SHAPING IT INTO PACKAGES. AS LONG AS THE CHEESE IS WRAPPED IN A DOUBLE THICKNESS OF OVERLAPPING PHYLLO, IT SHOULD NOT SEEP OUT DURING BAKING.

8 sheets of phyllo pastry
about 4 tablespoons butter, melted
3 tablespoons homemade (see page 249) or store-bought red pesto
8 oz mozzarella cheese, sliced
½ cup vegetarian Parmesan-style cheese, grated
salt and black pepper
leafy salad, to serve

Serves **4**
Prep time **15 minutes**
Cooking time **10 minutes**

AFFORDABILITY **1**

1 Cut two squares from each sheet of phyllo pastry. Lay eight squares on a clean work surface and brush with a little melted butter. Cover each with a second square to make a total of eight pastry stacks.

2 Dot a little pesto into the center of each pastry stack and spread slightly. Arrange the cheese over the pesto. Season lightly with salt and black pepper.

3 Bring two opposite sides of one of the pastry stacks over the filling to enclose completely. Lightly brush with butter, then fold over the two open ends to make a package. Place it on a baking sheet with the ends uppermost. Repeat with the remaining pastry stacks.

4 Brush with the remaining butter (melt a little more if necessary) and bake in a preheated oven, at 400°F, for about 10 minutes, until golden. Serve warm with a leafy salad.

Tofu & Honey PACKAGES

1 Melt half of the butter in a skillet, add the onions, and sauté for 3 minutes, until softened. Stir in the slivered almonds and sauté for 2 minutes, until turning golden. Stir in the honey, cinnamon, and tofu, then season to taste with salt and black pepper.

2 Melt the remaining butter in a small saucepan. Cut out 16 squares from the phyllo pastry. Lay eight squares on a clean work surface and brush with a little melted butter. Cover each with a second square placed at an angle to create a star shape. Pile the tofu mixture onto the centers of the squares.

3 Brush the edges of the pastry with a little butter. Bring the edges up over the filling and pinch together to make bundles. Repeat with the remaining pastries. Transfer to a baking sheet and brush with the remaining butter.

4 Bake in a preheated oven, at 400°F, for about 10 minutes, until the pastry is golden. Serve warm.

4 tablespoons butter
2 onions, chopped
½ cup slivered almonds, lightly crushed
1 tablespoon honey
1 teaspoon ground cinnamon
7 oz tofu, diced
8 sheets of phyllo pastry
salt and black pepper

Serves 4
Prep time 15 minutes
Cooking time 15 minutes

AFFORDABILITY
1

LEEK & MUSHROOM PASTRIES

4 tablespoons butter
2 leeks, trimmed and sliced
1 lb white mushrooms, halved
   or quartered, if large
   (about 6½ cups)
1 cup cream cheese
1 teaspoon dried tarragon or
   1 tablespoon chopped fresh
   tarragon
1 (1 lb) package puff pastry,
   thawed if frozen
flour, for dusting
beaten egg, to glaze
salt and black pepper

Serves 4
Prep time **15 minutes**
Cooking time **25-30 minutes**

1 Melt the butter in a large skillet, add the leeks, and sauté over medium heat for 3 minutes, stirring occasionally, until they begin to soften. Add the mushrooms and continue to sauté for another 4-5 minutes, until tender and lightly golden, then stir in the cream cheese and tarragon.

2 Meanwhile, roll out the pastry on a lightly floured surface and cut out four 8 inch circles. Brush a ½ inch border with a little beaten egg.

3 Season the leek and mushrooms with a pinch each of salt and black pepper, then divide the mixture among the pastry circles. Now bring up two sides of the pastry to encase the filling, crimping the pastry together with your fingers to seal the edges. Repeat to make four pastries.

4 Place the pastries on a baking sheet, brush with the remaining beaten egg, and cook in a preheated oven, at 400°F, for about 18 minutes, until puffed up and golden. Serve warm.

AFFORDABILITY 1

Red Onion
& GOAT CHEESE *Tart*

1 Melt the butter in a large skillet, add the onions, sugar, and chopped thyme, and cook gently for 20 minutes, stirring occasionally, until the onions start to caramelize. Stir in the vinegar and cook for 1 minute. Let cool slightly.

2 Unroll the pastry sheet and place on a nonstick baking sheet. Using a sharp knife, score a line along each side of the sheet 1 inch from the edge, being careful not to cut all the way through the pastry.

3 Spoon the caramelized onions over the pastry, within the scored border, then top with the goat cheese slices. Bake in a preheated oven, at 400°F, for 20 minutes, until the pastry is risen and golden. Serve garnished with a few thyme leaves.

2 tablespoons butter
4 large red onions, thinly sliced
1 teaspoon packed light brown sugar
2 tablespoons chopped thyme, plus a few extra leaves to garnish
2 teaspoons balsamic vinegar
1 sheet of ready-rolled puff pastry, thawed if frozen
2 (4 oz) round goat cheeses, each sliced into 4

Serves **4**
Prep time **10 minutes, plus cooling**
Cooking time **40 minutes**

AFFORDABILITY

MARGHERITA TART

1 Unroll the sheet of pastry on a lined or lightly greased baking sheet and lightly score a ¾ inch border around the edge.

2 Spread the pesto evenly over the pastry, working within the scored border. Arrange the cherry tomatoes and mozzarella over the pesto, then sprinkle with the olives and oregano, if using.

3 Drizzle with the oil and bake in a preheated oven, at 375°F, for 20-25 minutes, until the pastry is crisp and golden. Cut into squares and serve with an arugula salad, if desired.

1 sheet of ready-rolled puff pastry, thawed if frozen
2 teaspoons olive oil, plus extra for greasing
3 tablespoons homemade (see page 249) or store-bought green or red pesto
2 cups cherry tomatoes, halved (or 3 regular tomatoes, sliced)
4 oz mozzarella cheese, torn or sliced
12 pitted green or black ripe olives, rinsed and drained (optional)
1 teaspoon dried oregano (optional)
arugula salad, to serve (optional)

Serves **4**
Prep time **5 minutes**
Cooking time **20-25 minutes**

TOMATO TARTS
WITH CREAMY PESTO TOPPING

1 Lightly oil a large baking sheet and sprinkle with water. Heat the oil in a skillet, add the onion, and sauté for about 3 minutes, until softened. Halve about 1 cup of the tomatoes. Remove the pan from the heat, add the garlic and tomato paste, then stir in all the tomatoes, turning until they are lightly coated in the sauce.

2 Roll out the pastry on a lightly floured surface and cut out four 5 inch circles, using a cutter or small bowl as a guide. Transfer to the baking sheet and make a shallow cut ½ inch from the edge of each circle, using the tip of a sharp knife to form a rim. (Do not cut all the way through the pastry.) Brush the rims with beaten egg. Pile the tomato mixture into the centers of the pastries, making sure the mixture stays within the rims. Bake in a preheated oven, at 425°F, for about 15 minutes, until the pastry is risen and golden.

3 Meanwhile, lightly mix together the yogurt, pesto, and salt and black pepper in a bowl so that the yogurt is streaked with the pesto.

4 Transfer the cooked tarts to warmplates and spoon over the creamy pesto. Serve sprinkled with basil leaves.

2 tablespoons olive oil, plus extra for greasing
1 onion, finely chopped
2½ cups cherry tomatoes
2 garlic cloves, crushed
3 tablespoons tomato paste
1 sheet of puff pastry, thawed if frozen
flour, for dusting
beaten egg, to glaze
⅔ cup plain Greek yogurt
2 tablespoons homemade (see page 249) or store-bought pesto
salt and black pepper
basil leaves, to garnish

Serves **4**
Prep time **10 minutes**
Cooking time **20 minutes**

AFFORDABILITY 1

Cheese & Tomato Muffins with Basil

1 Lightly oil eight cups of a muffin pan. Sift the flour, baking powder, and salt into a bowl and stir in the cornmeal, ½ cup of the cheese, the tomatoes, and basil. Make a well in the center.

2 Beat the egg, milk, and oil together in a separate bowl, pour into the well, and stir together until just combined. The batter should remain a little lumpy.

3 Divide the batter among the cups of the muffin pan and sprinkle the remaining 2 tablespoons of cheese over them. Bake in a preheated oven, at 350°F, for 20-25 minutes, until risen and golden. Let cool in the pan for 5 minutes, then transfer to a wire rack to cool. Serve warm with butter.

2 tablespoons olive oil, plus extra for greasing
1¼ cups all-purpose flour
1¼ teaspoons baking powder
½ teaspoon salt
¾ cup fine cornmeal
⅔ cup shredded cheddar cheese
½ cup chopped, drained sun-dried tomatoes in oil
2 tablespoons chopped basil
1 egg, lightly beaten
1¼ cups milk
butter, to serve

Makes 8
Prep time 10 minutes
Cooking time 20-25 minutes

AFFORDABILITY 2

CHEESE & HERB
BISCUITS

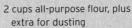

2 cups all-purpose flour, plus
  extra for dusting
2 teaspoons baking powder
6 tablespoons unsalted butter,
  diced
¼ cup vegetarian grated
  Parmesan-style cheese
3 tablespoons chopped mixed
  fresh herbs, such as oregano
  and chives
1 egg, lightly beaten
2 tablespoons buttermilk

Makes **12**
Prep time **10 minutes**
Cooking time **10-12 minutes**

1 Sift the flour and baking powder into a large bowl, add the butter, and rub in with the fingertips until the mixture resembles fine bread crumbs. Add 3 tablespoons of the cheese and the herbs and stir together.

2 Beat together the egg and buttermilk in a separate bowl. Use a knife or fork to combine the wet and dry ingredients lightly and bring them together to form a ball.

3 Shape the dough into a circle, about 1 inch thick, and press out 12 circles with a plain 2 inch cutter. Place the biscuits on a lightly floured baking sheet and sprinkle with the reserved cheese.

4 Bake in a preheated oven, at 425°F, for 10-12 minutes, until golden and well risen. The biscuits can be stored in an airtight container for up to 3 days.

Quick
MEDITERRANEAN
FOCACCIA

olive oil, for brushing
3²/₃ cups all-purpose flour,
  plus extra for dusting
1 teaspoon baking soda
1 teaspoon salt
1 tablespoon chopped
  rosemary, plus 10 small
  sprigs
1 cup chopped sun-dried
  tomatoes
1³/₄ cups buttermilk
10 pitted black ripe olives
1 teaspoon sea salt

Serves 8
Prep time **15 minutes**
Cooking time **15 minutes**

1 Brush a 9 inch x 12½ inch jellyroll pan generously with oil.

2 Sift the flour, baking soda, and salt into a large bowl. Stir in the chopped rosemary and sun-dried tomatoes. Make a well in the center, add the buttermilk to the well, and gradually stir into the flour. Bring the mixture together with your hands to form a soft, slightly sticky dough.

3 Turn out the dough onto a lightly floured surface and lightly knead for 1 minute, then quickly roll into a rectangular shape to fit the pan. Press the dough gently into the pan, then brush with oil. Using your finger, make small dimples in the top of the bread. Sprinkle with the olives, rosemary sprigs, and sea salt.

4 Bake in a preheated oven, at 425°F, for 15 minutes, until brown and crisp. Brush with a little more olive oil and serve warm.

AFFORDABILITY
1

SPICED
Flatbreads

1 Toast the cumin and coriander seeds in a dry skillet over medium heat until aromatic, then crush with a mortar and pestle. Alternatively, put the cooled seeds into a plastic food bag and crush with the back of a spoon.

2 Mix together the flour, yeast, sugar, salt, and toasted spices in a large bowl. Make a well in the center, add the oil to the well, and gradually stir into the flour with enough of about 1 cup warm water to form a moist, pliable dough.

3 Turn out the dough onto a lightly floured surface and knead for 5 minutes, until smooth and elastic. Divide into four balls and roll out thinly on a lightly floured surface into long oval or round shapes. Prick all over with a fork and arrange on nonstick baking sheets.

4 Bake in a preheated oven, at 425°F, for 3 minutes. Turn the breads over and bake for another 3 minutes, until golden brown. Serve immediately or wrap in a clean dish towel or aluminum foil to keep warm before serving.

2 teaspoons cumin seeds
1 teaspoon coriander seeds
3⅓ cups white bread flour, plus extra for dusting
2¼ teaspoons or 1 (¼ oz) envelope active dry yeast
1 teaspoon sugar
1 teaspoon sea salt
1 tablespoon olive oil

....

Makes 4
Prep time 15 minutes
Cooking time 8 minutes

....

Mixed Seed SODA BREAD

vegetable oil, for greasing
2¾ cups whole wheat flour, plus extra for dusting and sprinkling
⅓ cup sunflower seeds
2 tablespoons poppy seeds
1 teaspoon baking soda
1 teaspoon salt
1 teaspoon sugar
1¼ cups buttermilk

Makes **1 small loaf**
Prep time **10 minutes**
Cooking time **40-45 minutes**

1 Lightly oil a baking sheet. Mix together the flour, sunflower seeds, poppy seeds, baking soda, salt, and sugar in a bowl. Make a well in the center, add the buttermilk, and gradually work into the flour mixture to form a soft dough.

2 Turn out the dough onto a lightly floured work surface and knead for 5 minutes. Shape into a flattish circle. Transfer to the baking sheet. Using a sharp knife, cut a cross in the top of the bread. Sprinkle a little extra flour over the surface.

3 Bake in a preheated oven, at 450°F, for 15 minutes, then reduce the temperature to 400°F and bake for another 25-30 minutes, until risen and the loaf sounds hollow when tapped underneath. Let cool completely on a wire rack.

AFFORDABILITY
1

BLACKBERRY
Loaf Cake

THIS CAKE IS BEST EATEN FRESHLY MADE, PREFERABLY SLIGHTLY WARM.

1 stick unsalted butter, melted,
   plus extra for greasing
¾ cup milk
1 egg
2 cups all-purpose flour
2 teaspoons baking powder
¾ cup sugar, plus extra
   for dusting
⅓ cup rolled oats
¾ cup fresh blackberries

Serves 6-8
Prep time **10 minutes**
Cooking time **50-60 minutes**

1 Grease and line the bottom and sides of an 8½ x 4½ x 2½ inch loaf pan so that the paper comes about ½ inch above the rim of the pan. Grease the paper.

2 Beat together the butter, milk, and egg in a bowl. Sift the flour and baking powder into a separate bowl and stir in the sugar, oats, and half the blackberries. Stir the wet ingredients into the dry ingredients until only just combined.

3 Turn the batter into the pan and sprinkle with the remaining blackberries. Bake in a preheated oven, at 350°F, for 50-60 minutes or until well risen, golden, and firm to the touch. Let cool in the pan for 5 minutes, then transfer to a wire rack and sprinkle with a little extra sugar. Serve warm or cold.

AFFORDABILITY
1

COOKING TIP

When berries, such as strawberries and blackberries, are in season in the summer and a bargain, you can freeze them to use later on when the season has passed and their prices skyrocket. To freeze berries, spread them out in a single layer on a baking sheet and lay flat in the freezer. Once frozen, transfer to freezer bags and they won't stick together.

Lemon
DRIZZLE CAKE

2 sticks unsalted butter, softened, plus extra for greasing
1²/₃ cups sugar
finely grated zest of 3 lemons, plus ½ cup lemon juice
4 eggs, beaten
2 cups all-purpose flour
1 tablespoon baking powder
¾ cup ground almonds

Serves 8-10
Prep time **20 minutes**
Cooking time **45 minutes**

1 Grease and line the bottom and sides of an 8 inch round cake pan or a 7 inch square pan. Grease the paper.

2 Beat together the butter, 1 cup plus 2 tablespoons of the sugar, and the lemon zest in a bowl until light and fluffy. Beat in the eggs, a little at a time, beating well between each addition. Add a little of the flour if the mixture starts to curdle.

3 Sift the flour and baking powder into the bowl, add the ground almonds and 2 tablespoons of the lemon juice, and gently fold in, using a large metal spoon.

4 Turn the batter into the pan and level the surface. Bake in a preheated oven, at 350°F, for about 45 minutes or until just firm and a toothpick inserted into the center comes out clean.

5 Meanwhile, mix together the remaining lemon juice with the remaining sugar. Transfer the cake to a wire rack. Give the lemon mixture a good stir and spoon it over the cake. As the cake cools, the syrup will sink into the cake, leaving a sugary crust.

Strawberry LAYER CAKE

SANDWICH SIMPLY WITH PRESERVES FOR AN AFTERNOON TREAT OR, FOR A MORE DECADENT FILLING, SPREAD WITH PRESERVES AND 2/3 CUP WHIPPED CREAM.

1 Grease and line the bottoms of two 7 inch round cake pans.

2 Beat together the butter and sugar in a bowl until pale, light, and fluffy. Beat in the eggs, a little at a time, beating well after each addition. Add a little of the flour if the mixture starts to curdle.

3 Sift the flour and baking powder into the bowl and gently fold in, using a large metal spoon. Don't beat it or overmix or you will knock out all the air.

4 Divide the batter between the pans and level the surface. Bake in a preheated oven, at 350°F, for about 25 minutes or until risen and just firm to the touch. Loosen the edges of the cakes and turn out onto a wire rack to cool.

5 Sandwich the cakes together with the preserves and sprinkle generously with confectioners' sugar or spread with buttercream.

1½ sticks unsalted butter, softened, plus extra for greasing
¾ cup plus 2 tablespoons granulated sugar
3 eggs, beaten
1⅓ cups all-purpose flour
1½ teaspoons baking powder
⅓ cup strawberry or raspberry preserves
confectioners' sugar or Buttercream (see page 251)

Serves 8
Prep time **20 minutes**
Cooking time **25 minutes**

Vegan Banana Pecan Cake
WITH CARAMEL TOPPING

1 Lightly oil and line a loaf pan with a bottom measurement of about 7 x 3¾ inches. Lightly oil the paper.

2 Mash the bananas in a bowl and stir in the oil until evenly combined. Sift the flour, baking powder, and cinnamon into the bowl and add the sugar, nuts, and dried fruit.

3 Stir the ingredients together until well mixed and turn into the pan. Bake in a preheated oven, at 350°F, for 30 minutes, until slightly risen and just firm to the touch. Transfer to a wire rack to cool.

4 For the topping, put half the milk into a saucepan with the sugar and heat until the sugar dissolves. Bring to a boil and boil for 4-5 minutes, until the syrup starts to turn golden around the edges. Meanwhile, blend the cornstarch into the remaining milk and mix until smooth. Add to the saucepan and cook, stirring, for 2-3 minutes, until thickened. Let cool before spreading over the cake and sprinkling with extra nuts.

3 tablespoons vegetable oil, plus extra for greasing
2 small ripe bananas
1 cup all-purose flour
1½ teaspoons baking powder
½ teaspoon ground cinnamon
¼ cup packed light brown sugar
½ cup pecans, chopped, plus extra to decorate
3 tablespoons golden raisins or raisins

Caramel topping
½ cup unsweetened almond milk
¼ cup granulated sugar
1 teaspoon cornstarch

Serves **6**
Prep time **15 minutes**, plus cooling
Cooking time **40 minutes**

CHOCOLATE
Fudge Cake

THIS IS A RICH, CHOCOLATE-PACKED CAKE WITH
NOT THE FAINTEST HINT OF DRYNESS.

1 Grease and line the bottoms of three 8 inch cake pans.
(If you only have two pan, bake one-third of the cake
batter afterward.)

2 Whisk the cocoa powder in a bowl with 1¼ cups boiling
water until smooth. Stir in the chopped chocolate and let
cool, stirring occasionally.

3 Beat together the butter, sugar, flour, baking powder, and
eggs in a bowl until smooth. Beat in the chocolate mixture.

4 Divide the batter evenly among the pans and level
the surface. Bake in a preheated oven, at 350°F, for
20-25 minutes or until just firm to the touch. Transfer to
a wire rack to cool.

5 Make the frosting. Melt the chocolate in a
small heatproof bowl set over a saucepan
of simmering water (do not let the bowl touch the
water). Remove from the heat and let cool slightly.
Beat the confectiones' sugar and butter together
until creamy, then beat in the chocolate until
smooth. Use the frosting to sandwich the cake
layers on a serving plate. Pile the remainder on top,
spreading it evenly with a spatula over the cake.

1¾ sticks unsalted butter,
  softened, plus extra for
  greasing
1 cup plus 2 tablespoons
  unsweetened cocoa powder
4 oz semisweet chocolate,
  chopped
1½ cups packed light brown sugar
2¼ cups all-purpose flour
2¾ teaspoons baking powder
3 eggs, beaten

Fudge frosting
10 oz semisweet chocolate,
  broken up
1¾ cups confectioners' sugar
1¾ sticks unsalted butter,
  softened

Serves 12
Prep time **25 minutes,**
plus cooling
Cooking time **20-25 minutes**

LEMON POPPING
Candy Cakes

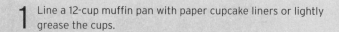

1 stick unsalted butter, softened, plus extra for greasing
²⁄₃ cup granulated sugar
1 cup all-purpose flour
1 teaspoons baking powder
2 eggs
1 tablespoon milk
2 teaspoons finely grated lemon zest
1¼ cups confectioners' sugar, sifted
about 2 teaspoons lemon juice
popping candy (available online) or sugar sprinkles, to sprinkle

Makes 12
Prep time **15 minutes, plus cooling**
Cooking time **12-15 minutes**

1 Line a 12-cup muffin pan with paper cupcake liners or lightly grease the cups.

2 Beat together the butter, sugar, flour, baking powder, eggs, milk, and 1 teaspoon of the lemon zest in a bowl until pale and creamy.

3 Divide the batter evenly among the liners or cups of the muffin pan and bake in a preheated oven, at 375°F, for 12-15 minutes, until golden and risen. Transfer to a wire rack to cool.

4 Meanwhile, mix the confectioners' sugar with the remaining lemon zest and just enough lemon juice to create a thick, smooth icing. Spread over the cold cupcakes and sprinkle with popping candy.

AFFORDABILITY

VEGAN CHILI & LIME
Chocolate Muffins

(V)

1 Line a muffin pan with 10 paper muffin liners.

2 Sift the flour, baking powder, chili powder, and cocoa powder into a bowl. Stir in the sugar and salt. Mix together the lime zest, vegetable oil, milk, and vanilla extract in a separate bowl. Add to the dry ingredients and stir together until combined.

3 Spoon the batter into the muffin liners so they're almost full. Bake in a preheated oven, at 375°F, for 20 minutes, until risen and just firm to the touch. Turn off the oven and let the muffins cool in the oven.

4 For the glaze, put the sugar, cocoa powder, lime juice, and 2 tablespoons water in a small saucepan and heat gently until the sugar dissolves. Bring to a boil and boil for 30-60 seconds until slightly thickened. Drizzle over the muffins.

1²/₃ cups all-purpose flour
1½ teaspoons baking powder
¼ teaspoon chili powder
1 cup unsweetened cocoa
  powder
1 cup packed light brown sugar
good pinch of salt
finely grated zest of 2 limes
²/₃ cup vegetable oil
½ cup unsweetened almond
  milk or soy milk
1 teaspoon vanilla extract

Glaze
2 tablespoons packed light
  brown sugar
1 tablespoon unsweetened
  cocoa powder
1 tablespoon lime juice

Makes **10**
Prep time **15 minutes,**
plus cooling
Cooking time **25 minutes**

Chocolate
MOCHA BROWNIES

LIKE ALL THE BEST BROWNIE RECIPES, THIS VERSION'S BOTH GOOEY AND FUDGY. TRY TO RESIST THE TEMPTATION TO OVERINDULGE—THEY ARE PACKED WITH CHOCOLATE AND INCREDIBLY RICH.

1 Grease and line a shallow 11 x 7 inch rectangular baking pan or a 9 inch square baking pan.

2 Melt the semisweet chocolate with the butter in a heatproof bowl set over a saucepan of simmering water (do not let the bowl touch the water), stirring frequently, until smooth. Stir in the coffee.

3 In a separate bowl, beat together the eggs and sugar. Stir in the melted chocolate mixture, sift the flour and baking powder into the bowl and stir until they are combined.

4 Add the chopped milk chocolate and turn the batter into the pan. Level the surface and bake in a preheated oven, at 375°F, for about 30 minutes or until a crust has formed but the brownies feels soft underneath. Let cool in the pan, then cut into squares.

1½ sticks unsalted butter, plus extra for greasing
8 oz semisweet chocolate, broken up
2 tablespoons instant coffee
3 eggs
1 cup packed light brown sugar
⅔ cup all-purpose flour
½ teaspoon baking powder
7 oz milk chocolate, coarsely chopped

....

Makes **15**
Prep time **15 minutes**
Cooking time **30 minutes**

....

CHOCOLATE
CHIP COOKIES

1 Line a large baking sheet with nonstick parchment paper.

2 Beat the butter and sugar together in a large bowl until light and fluffy. Mix in the vanilla extract, then gradually beat in the egg, beating well after each addition. Stir in the milk.

3 Sift the flour and baking powder into a separate large bowl, then fold into the butter and egg mixture. Stir in the chocolate chips.

4 Drop level tablespoonfuls of the cookie mixture onto the baking sheet, leaving about 1½ inches between each cookie, then lightly press with a floured fork. Bake in a preheated oven, at 350°F4, for 15 minutes or until lightly golden. Transfer to a wire rack to cool.

1 stick unsalted butter, softened
¾ cup packed light brown sugar
1 teaspoon vanilla extract
1 egg, lightly beaten
1 tablespoon milk
1²/₃ cups all-purpose flour
1 teaspoon baking powder
1½ cups semisweet chocolate chips

Makes **16**
Prep time **10 minutes**
Cooking time **15 minutes**

AFFORDABILITY 1

Energy Oat & RAISIN BARS

1 Grease and line the bottom of a 10 inch square baking pan with a depth of about 1½ inches.

2 Melt the butter with the corn syrup or honey, the condensed milk, and sugar in a large saucepan over medium-low heat, then remove from the heat and stir in the oats, raisins, flour, and baking powder. Stir well.

3 Scrape the batter into the pan and bake in a preheated oven, at 350°F, for 15-18 minutes, until pale golden in colour. Let cool in the pan for 2-3 minutes.

4 Cut about 16 squares or bars, then let cool in the pan for 5 minutes or until cool and firm enough to handle. Transfer to a wire rack.

1¾ sticks unsalted butter, plus extra for greasing
⅓ cup light corn syrup or honey
½ cup sweetened condensed milk
⅔ cup granulated sugar
4 cups rolled oats
½ cup raisins
⅔ cup all-purpose flour
½ teaspoon baking powder

Makes 16
Prep time **5 minutes**
Cooking time **18-20 minutes**

AFFORDABILITY
2

CRUMBLY
RASPBERRY & OAT SLICES

1¾ sticks unsalted butter,
  slightly softened and diced,
  plus extra for greasing
¾ cup all-purpose flour
⅔ cup whole wheat flour
2 cups rolled oats
¾ cup granulated sugar
finely grated zest of 1 lemon
2 cups fresh or frozen
  raspberries
confectioners' sugar,
  for dusting

Makes 12-14
Prep time 15 minutes
Cooking time 1 hour

1 Lightly grease the bottom and sides of a shallow 10½ x 7 inch rectangular baking pan or roasting pan.

2 Place the flours and oats in a bowl, add the butter, and rub in with the fingertips until the mixture resembles coarse bread crumbs. Stir in the sugar and lemon zest and continue to crumble the mixture together until it starts to cling together.

3 Turn half the batter into the pan and pat it down into an even layer. Spread the raspberries on top and sprinkle with the remaining crumb mixture.

4 Bake in a preheated oven, at 350°F, for about 1 hour or until the topping is turning golden. Cut into fingers and let cool in the pan. Serve dusted with confectioners' sugar.

AFFORDABILITY
2

CRANBERRY & OATMEAL SCONES

LIKE BISCUITS, THESE SWEET FRUIT-SPECKED SCONES ARE BEST SERVED FRESHLY BAKED, OR FROZEN AHEAD AND THEN WARMED THROUGH TO SERVE.

6 tablespoons unsalted butter, diced, plus extra for greasing
1⅓ cups all-purpose flour, plus extra for dusting
2¼ teaspoons baking powder
1 teaspoon ground cinnamon
⅓ cup sugar
⅔ cup rolled oats, plus extra for sprinkling
½ cup dried cranberries
5-6 tablespoons milk
beaten egg or milk, to glaze

Makes 10
Prep time 10 minutes
Cooking time 10-12 minutes

1 Grease a baking sheet.

2 Put the flour, baking powder, and cinnamon into a bowl, add the butter, and rub in with the fingertips until the mixture resembles bread crumbs. Stir in the sugar and oats. Add the cranberries and milk and stir briefly until the batter forms a soft dough, adding a little more milk, if necessary.

3 Turn out onto a floured surface and roll out to ¾ inch thick. Cut out circles using a 2 inch cutter. Transfer to the baking sheet and reroll the scraps to make 10 scones.

4 Brush with beaten egg or milk and sprinkle with oats. Bake in a preheated oven, at 425°F, for 10-12 minutes, until risen and golden. Transfer to a wire rack to cool. Serve split and buttered.

AFFORDABILITY 1

STIR-FRIED TOFU

Made in a Flash

KALE & PESTO LINGUINE

MANGO CURRY

CORN CAKES
WITH AVOCADO SALSA

1 Put three-quarters of the corn kernels along with the scallions, eggs, cilantro, flour, and baking powder into a food processor or blender and process until combined. Alternatively, blend the ingredients, in batches, using an immersion blender. Season well and transfer to a large bowl. Add the remaining corn kernels and mix well.

2 Heat 1 tablespoon of the oil in a large, nonstick skillet over medium-high heat. When the oil is hot, drop heaping tablespoons of the batter into the pan and cook for 1 minute on each side. Drain on paper towels and keep warm in a low oven while cooking the remaining batter in the same way.

3 To make the avocado salsa, put all the ingredients into a bowl and stir gently to combine. Serve the warm corn cakes garnished with cilantro leaves, with the tangy avocado salsa on the side.

3⅓ cups corn kernels, thawed if frozen
4 scallions, finely sliced
2 eggs
⅓ cup finely chopped cilantro leaves, plus extra to garnish
1 cup all-purpose flour
1 teaspoon baking powder
salt and black pepper
vegetable oil, for frying

Avocado salsa
2 ripe avocados, peeled, pitted, and finely diced
¼ cup each of chopped mint and cilantro leaves
2 tablespoons lime juice
2 tablespoons finely chopped red onion
½ teaspoon Tabasco sauce

Serves **4**
Prep time **15 minutes**
Cooking time **10 minutes**

Tricolore AVOCADO & COUSCOUS Salad

1 cup couscous
1¼ cups hot Vegetable Broth (see page 246) or boiling water
2 cups cherry tomatoes
2 avocados, peeled, pitted, and chopped
1½ cups chopped mozzarella cheese
handful of arugula leaves

Dressing
2 tablespoons homemade (see page 249) or store-bought pesto
1 tablespoon lemon juice
¼ cup olive oil
salt and black pepper

Serves **4**
Prep time **10 minutes, plus standing**

1 Mix the couscous and broth or water together in a bowl, then cover with a plate and let stand for 10 minutes.

2 To make the dressing, mix the pesto with the lemon juice and season, then gradually mix in the oil. Pour it over the couscous and mix with a fork.

3 Add the tomatoes, avocados, and mozzarella to the couscous, mix well, then lightly stir in the arugula.

Bulgur Wheat
WITH GOAT CHEESE & RED ONION

3 cups hot Vegetable Broth
(see page 246)
2 cups bulgur wheat
¼ cup vegetable oil
1 large red onion, halved and
thinly sliced
½ cup tomato juice
2 tablespoons lime juice
6 oz firm goat cheese, crumbled
3 tablespoons coarsely chopped
flat leaf parsley
salt and black pepper

Serves 4
Prep time **10 minutes**
Cooking time **15 minutes**

1 Bring the broth to a boil in a large saucepan, add the bulgar wheat, and cook for 7 minutes. Remove from the heat, cover with a tight-fitting lid, and set aside for 5-8 minutes, until the liquid has been absorbed and the grains are tender.

2 Meanwhile, heat 2 tablespoons of oil in a skillet, add the onion, and sauté gently for 7-8 minutes, until soft and golden.

3 Combine the remaining oil with the tomato juice and lime juice, then season with salt and black pepper. Fold the dressing, onion, goat cheese, and parsley into the bulgur wheat with a fork, then spoon into warm shallow bowls to serve.

CORN & BEAN
TORTILLA STACK

1 Heat the oil in a large saucepan, add the chopped bell peppers, cover with a lid, and cook gently for 5 minutes. Add the tomatoes, beans, corn, and chili powder. Bring to a boil and simmer, uncovered, for 7–8 minutes, until the mixture is thick.

2 Place one tortilla on a baking sheet. Top with one-third of the bean mixture and one-quarter of the cheese. Repeat this twice to make three layers and then place the final tortilla on top. Sprinkle with the remaining cheese and bake in a preheated oven, at 375°F, for 15 minutes.

3 Garnish with the chopped cilantro leaves and serve with avocado and sour cream, if desired.

2 tablespoons vegetable oil
2 red bell peppers, cored, seeded, and chopped
1 (14½ oz) can diced tomatoes
2 (15 oz) cans kidney beans, drained
1 (15¼ oz) can corn kernels, drained
½ teaspoon chili powder
4 large corn tortillas
2 cups shredded cheddar cheese
1 tablespoon finely chopped cilantro leaves, to garnish

To serve
sour cream (optional)
1 avocado, peeled, pitted, and sliced (optional)

Serves **4**
Prep time **15 minutes**
Cooking time **30 minutes**

AFFORDABILITY 2

FALAFEL CAKES

THESE TASTY CHICKPEA CAKES, TRADITIONALLY ROLLED INTO LITTLE BALLS AND DEEP-FRIED, MAKE A GREAT VEGGIE DINNER SERVED SIMPLY WITH A FRESH, GREEK-STYLE SALAD.

1 (15 oz) can chickpeas, rinsed and drained
1 onion, coarsely chopped
3 garlic cloves, coarsely chopped
2 teaspoons cumin seeds
1 teaspoon mild chili powder
2 tablespoons chopped mint
3 tablespoons chopped fresh cilantro
1 cup fresh bread crumbs
vegetable oil, for pan-frying
salt and black pepper

Serves 4
Prep time **10 minutes**
Cooking time **10 minutes**

1 Using an immersion blender, or a food processor or blender if you have one, briefly blend the chickpeas with the onion, garlic, spices, herbs, bread crumbs, and a little salt and black pepper to make a chunky paste.

2 Take tablespoonfuls of the mixture and flatten into cakes. Heat a ½ inch depth of oil in a skillet and cook half the falafel for about 3 minutes, turning once until crisp and golden. Drain on paper towels and keep warm while cooking the remainder in the same way.

AFFORDABILITY 1

COOKING TIP

Don't throw away the crusts of bread—you can process dry, stale bread in a food processor (try using an immersion blender or a cheese grater if you don't have a processor) and keep in a sealed bag in the freezer. That way you always have a ready supply of bread crumbs for casserole toppings and burger mixes.

NUT KEBABS
with Minted Yogurt

5–6 tablespoons vegetable oil
1 onion, chopped
½ teaspoon dried red pepper
flakes
2 garlic cloves, coarsely
chopped
1 tablespoon medium curry
paste (suitable for
vegetarians)
1 (15 oz) can cranberry or
cannellini (white kidney)
beans, rinsed and drained
1¼ cups ground almonds
(almond meal)
¾ cup chopped honey-roast
or salted almonds
1 medium egg
flour, for dusting
1 cup Greek yogurt
2 tablespoons chopped mint
1 tablespoon lemon juice
salt and black pepper
warm naan or other flatbread,
to serve
mint sprigs, to garnish

Serves 4
Prep time **15 minutes**
Cooking time **10 minutes**

1 Soak eight bamboo skewers in hot water while preparing the kebabs. Alternatively, use metal skewers that do not require presoaking.

2 Heat 3 tablespoons of the oil in a skillet, add the onion, and sauté for 4 minutes. Add the red pepper flakes, garlic, and curry paste and sauté for 1 minute. Transfer to a food processor or blender with the beans, ground almonds, chopped almonds, egg, and a little salt and black pepper and process until the mixture starts to bind together. Alternatively, blend together in a bowl using an immersion blender—you may need to do this in batches.

3 Using lightly floured hands, take about one-eighth of the mixture and mold around a skewer, forming it into a cylinder about 1 inch thick. Make seven more kebabs in the same way. Place on an aluminum foil-lined broiler rack and brush with another 1 tablespoon of the oil. Cook under a preheated medium broiler for about 5 minutes, turning once, until golden.

4 Meanwhile, mix together the yogurt and mint in a small serving bowl and season to taste with salt and black pepper. In a separate bowl, mix together the remaining oil, lemon juice, and a little salt and black pepper.

5 Brush the kebabs with the lemon dressing and serve with the yogurt dressing on warm naan or other flatbread garnished with mint sprigs.

AFFORDABILITY
2

Ricotta & FAVA BEAN *Fritters*

1 Cook the fava beans in a saucepan of boiling water for 2 minutes to soften. Drain well and coarsely chop.

2 Put the beans in a bowl and beat in the shallot, ricotta, egg yolk, and capers. Stir in the flour and a little salt and black pepper. Whisk the egg white in a thoroughly clean bowl until it forms peaks. Gently stir the egg white into the bean mixture until just combined.

3 Mix together the ingredients for the dip and season lightly.

4 Heat a dash of oil in a skillet. Place tabnlespoonfuls of the batter in the pan and flatten slightly with the back of the spoon. Cook gently for 3-4 minutes, turning once, until golden. Drain on paper towels and keep warm while cooking the remainder in the same way. Serve with the dip and a leafy salad.

²⁄₃ cup frozen baby fava beans
1 shallot, grated or finely chopped
½ cup ricotta cheese
1 egg, separated
1 tablespoon capers, drained
⅓ cup all-purpose flour
vegetable oil, for frying
salt and black pepper
leafy salad, to serve

Yogurt dip
¼ cup Greek yogurt
1 small garlic clove, crushed
2 tablespoons chopped mint
finely grated zest of ½ lemon

Serves **2**
Prep time **15 minutes**
Cooking time **10 minutes**

AFFORDABILITY
1

COUSCOUS FRITTERS
WITH BEETS

¾ cup couscous
½ cup hot Vegetable Broth
  (see page 246)
4 scallions, finely chopped
2 garlic cloves, chopped
3 tablespoons chopped parsley,
  plus extra to garnish
½ cup pine nuts, coarsely
  chopped
¾ cup ground almonds
  (almond meal)
finely grated zest of 1 lemon
1 egg
vegetable oil, for frying
4 small cooked beets, cut into
  wedges
salt and black pepper
crème fraîche or plain Greek
  yogurt, to serve

Dressing
¼ cup olive oil
1 teaspoon Tabasco sauce
1 tablespoon lemon juice

Serves **4**
Prep time **15 minutes**
Cooking time **5 minutes**

1 Put two-thirds of the couscous into a bowl, add the broth, and let stand for 5 minutes. Meanwhile, mix together the ingredients for the dressing in a small bowl.

2 When the couscous has absorbed all the broth, fluff up with a fork and stir in the scallions, garlic, parsley, pine nuts, almonds, lemon zest, and egg. Season with salt and black pepper and mix until the ingredients bind together.

3 Take heaping teaspoonfuls of the mixture and shape into balls. Roll them in the remaining couscous. Wet your hands before rolling the balls if the mixture starts to stick.

4 Heat a 1 inch depth of oil in a skillet or heavy saucepan. Add half the couscous balls and cook for about 2 minutes, until golden. Drain on paper towels and keep warm while cooking the remainder in the same way.

5 Arrange the beet wedges on warm serving plates and pile the fritters beside them. Top with a spoonful of crème fraîche or yogurt, garnish with parsley, and serve with the dressing spooned over the top.

AFFORDABILITY
2

Grilled GREEK-STYLE SANDWICHES

1 Mix together the onion, tomatoes, olives, cucumber, oregano, and feta in a small bowl. Add the lemon juice, season to taste with black pepper, and gently mix.

2 Split each pita bread in half horizontally. Divide the feta mixture between the bottom halves of the pita breads, then add the cheddar or American cheese. Cover with the top halves of the pita breads.

3 Brush a skillet with oil and heat over medium heat. When hot, add the sandwiches, press down gently with a spatula, and cook for 2-3 minutes on each side, until golden and the cheese has melted. Serve immediately.

¼ small red onion, thinly sliced
8 cherry tomatoes, quartered
4 pitted black ripe olives, chopped
2 inch piece of cucumber, seeded and cut into small pieces
1 teaspoon dried oregano
⅓ cup crumbled feta cheese
1 teaspoon lemon juice
2 round seeded pita breads
¼ cup shredded cheddar or American cheese
olive oil, for brushing
black pepper

Serves **2**
Prep time **15 minutes**
Cooking time **4-6 minutes**

Smoky Bean & Cheese BURGERS

1 Thoroughly drain the beans and pat dry between several sheets of paper towels. Transfer to a bowl and mash coarsely with a fork. Add the carrot, scallions, bread crumbs, cheese, paprika, and a little salt and stir well to combine. Add the egg and mix to a thick paste.

2 Divide the mixture into four equal pieces and shape each into a patty. Heat the oil in a skillet and cook the patties for 3-4 minutes on each side, until browned and heated through.

3 Place handfuls of arugula leaves on the bun bottoms and position the burgers on top. Add tomato and chile slices and mayonnaise, then top with the bun lids to serve.

1 (15 oz) can black beans
1 small carrot, grated
2 scallions, finely chopped
1 cup fresh whole meal or white bread crumbs
¾ cup shredded Manchego, cheddar, or American cheese
1 teaspoon smoked paprika
1 egg, beaten
2 tablespoons vegetable oil
salt

To serve
arugula leaves
hamburger buns, split
tomato slices
sliced green jalapeño chiles
mayonnaise

Serves **4**
Prep time **15 minutes**
Cooking time **6-8 minutes**

AFFORDABILITY 1

BEAN BURGERS WITH
CUCUMBER SALSA

• •

¾ cup rinsed and drained
  canned lima beans
1 onion, finely chopped
1 carrot, shredded
1 cup shredded sharp cheddar
  or American cheese
2 cups fresh bread crumbs
1 egg
1 teaspoon cumin seeds
flour, for dusting
vegetable oil, for shallow-frying
4 round crusty rolls
salt and black pepper
salad, to serve

Salsa
½ small cucumber
2 tablespoons chopped fresh
  cilantro
2 scallions, finely chopped
1 tablespoon lemon or lime juice
1 teaspoon sugar

Serves **4**
Prep time **10 minutes**
Cooking time **8 minutes**

1 Put the lima beans into a bowl and lightly mash with a fork. Add the onion, carrot, cheese, bread crumbs, egg, cumin seeds, and salt and black pepper and mix until evenly combined.

2 Using lightly floured hands, shape the mixture into four small flat patties. Heat a little oil in a large skillet and cook the patties for about 8 minutes, turning once, until crisp and golden.

3 Meanwhile, make the salsa. Halve the cucumber and scoop out the seeds. Finely chop the cucumber and toss in a bowl with the cilantro, scallions, lemon or lime juice, sugar, and a little salt and black pepper.

4 Slice the rolls in half and sandwich the burgers and salsa between the halves. Serve with salad.

AFFORDABILITY
1

SCALLION CREPES
with Cream Cheese

1⅓ cups all-purpose flour
1 teaspoon baking powder
⅔ cup milk
2 extra-large eggs
4 tablespoons butter, melted
2 tablespoons each of finely
 chopped dill and chives,
 plus extra to garnish
4 scallions, finely chopped
vegetable oil, for pan-frying
salt and black pepper

To serve

1 cup cream cheese, whisked
 with juice of 1 lemon
2 plum tomatoes, finely
 chopped

Serves **4**
Prep time **10 minutes**
Cooking time **20-35 minutes**

1 Sift the flour and baking powder into a bowl with a pinch of salt. Whisk together the milk, eggs, butter, herbs, and scallions in a separate bowl. Stir the wet mixture into the dry ingredients until the mixture comes together as a smooth, thick batter (use a little less milk if you want thicker pancakes).

2 Heat a little vegetable oil in a small, nonstick skillet and spoon in one-eighth of the batter. Cook the crepe for 1-2 minutes or until bubbles form on the surface, then carefully turn it over and cook for another 1-2 minutes or until golden brown on both sides. Transfer to a plate and keep warm while cooking the remainder in the same way to make eight crepes.

3 Stack two crepes each on warm serving plates and spoon over a dollop of the cream cheese mixture. Top with the chopped tomatoes and serve garnished with a sprinkling of herbs and freshly ground black pepper.

AFFORDABILITY
1

Spinach & Potato TORTILLA

3 tablespoons vegetable oil
2 onions, finely chopped
2 russet potatoes, cooked, peeled, and cut into ½ inch cubes
2 garlic cloves, finely chopped
1 cup drained and coarsely chopped, cooked spinach
¼ cup finely chopped roasted red pepper
5 eggs
3-4 tablespoons shredded Manchego, cheddar, or American cheese
salt and black pepper

1 Heat the oil in a flameproof nonstick skillet, add the onions and potatoes, and cook over medium heat for 3-4 minutes or until the vegetables have softened but not browned, turning and stirring frequently. Add the garlic, spinach, and roasted pepper and stir to mix well.

2 Beat the eggs lightly and season well. Pour into the skillet, shaking the pan so that the egg evenly spreads. Cook gently for 8-10 minutes or until the tortilla is set at the bottom.

3 Sprinkle with the shredded cheese. Place the skillet under a preheated medium-hot broiler and cook for 3-4 minutes, until the top is set and golden. Remove from the heat, cut into bite-size squares or triangles, and serve warm or at room temperature.

Serves 4
Prep time 15 minutes
Cooking time 15-20 minutes

HALOUMI WITH POMEGRANATE
SALSA

1 First make the pomegranate salsa. Carefully scoop the pomegranate seeds into a bowl, discarding all the white membrane. Stir in the remaining ingredients and season with salt and black pepper.

2 Heat a large nonstick skillet for 2–3 minutes, until hot. Add the haloumi slices, in batches, and cook over high heat for about 60 seconds on each side, until browned and softened.

3 Meanwhile, warm the honey in a small saucepan until runny.

4 Transfer the pan-fried haloumi to warm serving plates and spoon the salsa over the cheese. Drizzle with the honey and salsa, then serve immediately.

1 lb haloumi or Muenster cheese, sliced
1 tablespoon honey

Pomegranate salsa
½ pomegranate
¼ cup olive oil
2 tablespoons chopped parsley
1 tablespoon lemon juice
1 small red chile, seeded and finely chopped
1 small garlic clove, crushed
1 teaspoon pomegranate syrup (optional)
salt and black pepper

Serves **4**
Prep time **10 minutes**
Cooking time **10 minutes**

Five-Minute PAD THAI (V)

1 Cook the noodles in a saucepan of boiling water for 3-4 minutes, or according to package directions, until tender.

2 Meanwhile, heat the oil in a skillet or wok, add the vegetables, and cook for about 4 minutes, stirring frequently, until softened.

3 Mix together the soy sauce, peanut butter, lemon or lime juice, red pepper flakes, sugar, and 2 tablespoons water. Drain the noodles and add to the pan with the sauce and peanuts. Stir well to combine and serve hot.

4 oz dried ribbon rice noodles
1 tablespoon peanut or vegetable oil
1 (12 oz) package prepared stir-fry vegetables with bean sprouts
2 tablespoons soy sauce
2 tablespoons chunky peanut butter
1 tablespoon lemon or lime juice
¼ teaspoon dried red pepper flakes
1 tablespoon packed light brown or granulated sugar
⅓ cup salted peanuts, coarsely chopped

Serves **2**
Prep time **3 minutes**
Cooking time **5 minutes**

STUDENT TIP

Convenience stores are exactly that— fine for when you need an emergency quart of milk or a chocolate fix, but definitely not the place to head to when you're doing the weekly shop. You'll pay a premium for the convenience factor and should make a beeline for superstores if you want to stretch your budget.

AFFORDABILITY
1

GINGERY BROILED TOFU *with* NOODLES

2 tablespoons vegetable oil
1 (16 oz) package prepared
  stir-fry vegetables
1 lb fresh noodles
14 oz firm tofu, thickly sliced

Marinade
1 inch piece of fresh ginger
  root, peeled and grated
2 large garlic cloves, crushed
3 tablespoons dark soy sauce
3 tablespoons honey

Serves 4
Prep time **5 minutes**
Cooking time **10 minutes**

1 Heat the oil in a skillet or wok, add the vegetables, and stir-fry for 3-4 minutes. Add the noodles and toss for another 3-4 minutes.

2 Meanwhile, mix together the ginger, garlic, soy, and honey. Add the sliced tofu and turn gently in the marinade to coat. Reserve the remaining marinade. Arrange the tofu on an aluminum foil-lined baking sheet and cook under a preheated medium broiler for about 4 minutes, carefully turning once, until golden.

3 Remove the noodles and vegetables from the heat, drizzle with the remaining marinade, and serve topped with the broiled tofu.

Stir-Fried Tofu
WITH GINGER & BASIL

2 tablespoons vegetable oil
12 oz firm tofu, cubed
2 inch piece of fresh ginger
  root, peeled and grated
2 garlic cloves, chopped
½ broccoli, trimmed and cut
  into bite-size pieces
4 cups sugar snap peas
⅔ cup Vegetable Broth
  (see page 246)
2 tablespoons sweet chili
  sauce
1 tablespoon light soy sauce
1 tablespoon dark soy sauce
1 tablespoon lime juice
2 teaspoons packed light
  brown sugar
handful of Thai basil leaves
rice or noodles, to serve

Serves **4**
Prep time **20 minutes**
Cooking time **6 minutes**

1 Heat half the oil in a skillet or wok until smoking, add the tofu, and stir-fry for 2–3 minutes, until golden all over. Remove with a slotted spoon.

2 Add the remaining oil to the pan, add the ginger and garlic, and stir-fry for 10 seconds, then add the broccoli and sugar snap peas and stir-fry for 1 minute.

3 Return the tofu to the pan and add the broth, chili sauce, soy sauces, lime juice, and sugar. Cook for 1 minute, until the vegetables are cooked but still crisp. Add the basil leaves and stir well. Serve immediately with rice or noodles.

AFFORDABILITY

SPINACH & MUSHROOM RAMEN

1 Heat the oil in a saucepan or wok, add the mushrooms, and sauté for 6-8 minutes, until golden. Add the scallions and garlic and sauté for another 1 minute.

2 Add the broth, red pepper flakes, and ginger and bring to a gentle simmer. Add the soy sauce, lemon juice, and sugar, stirring in to mix. When heated through, add the spinach, stirring it through until wilted.

3 Meanwhile, cook the noodles in a saucepan of boiling water for 3 minutes, or according to the package directions, until tender. Thoroughly drain the noodles into a warm serving bowl and ladle the soup on top to serve.

1 tablespoon peanut oil
   or vegetable oil
2 cups thinly sliced cremini
   mushrooms
½ bunch of scallions, sliced
   diagonally
1 garlic clove, sliced
1¼ cups Vegetable Broth
   (see page 246)
good pinch of dried red
   pepper flakes
½ inch piece of fresh ginger
   root, peeled and grated
1 tablespoon soy sauce
2 teaspoons lemon juice
1 teaspoon sugar
2 cups spinach, trimmed
4 oz Ramen noodles or egg
   noodles

Serves 1
Prep time **10 minutes**
Cooking time **12 minutes**

Thai Green Vegetable CURRY

2 red chiles (optional for spicier curry)
3 carrots
¼ butternut squash
1 tablespoon vegetable oil
3 tablespoons Thai green curry paste (suitable for vegetarians)
1¾ cups coconut milk
1 cup Vegetable Broth (see page 246)
6 kaffir lime leaves or 1 tablespoon finely grated lime zest
2 tablespoons soy sauce
1 tablespoon packed brown sugar
2 cups sugar snap peas
⅔ cup finely chopped cilantro leaves
juice of 1 lime
steamed jasmine rice, to serve

Serves **4**
Prep time **10 minutes**
Cooking time **12-16 minutes**

1 Seed and finely slice the chiles, if using. Peel the carrots and cut into thick batons. Peel and seed the butternut squash, then cut the flesh into ¾ inch cubes.

2 Heat the oil in a large nonstick wok or saucepan. Add the curry paste and chiles, if using, and stir-fry for 2-3 minutes.

3 Stir in the coconut milk, broth, lime leaves or lime zest, soy sauce, sugar, carrots, and butternut squash. Simmer, uncovered, for 6-8 minutes, stirring occasionally.

4 Add the sugar snaps and continue to simmer for 4-5 minutes. Remove from the heat and stir in the cilantro and lime juice. Serve with steamed jasmine rice.

Mango CURRY

1 tablespoon vegetable oil
1 teaspoon mustard seeds
1 onion, thinly sliced
15-20 curry leaves, fresh or
   dried
½ teaspoon dried red pepper
   flakes
1 teaspoon peeled and grated
   fresh ginger root
1 green chile, seeded and sliced
1 teaspoon turmeric
3 ripe mangoes, peeled, pitted,
   and thinly sliced
1¾ cups plain yogurt, lightly
   beaten
salt
warm chapattis or other
   flatbread, to serve

Serves 4
Prep time **10 minutes**
Cooking time **10 minutes**

1 Heat the oil in a large saucepan until hot, add the mustard seeds, onion, curry leaves, and red pepper flakes, and sauté, stirring, for 4-5 minutes or until the onion is lightly browned.

2 Add the ginger and chile and stir-fry for 1 minute, then add the turmeric and stir to mix well.

3 Remove the pan from the heat, add the mangoes and yogurt, and stir constantly until well mixed. Season to taste with salt.

4 Return the pan to low heat and heat through for 1 minute, stirring constantly. (Do not let it boil or the curry will curdle.) Serve immediately with warm chapattis or flatbread.

CREAMY Zucchini ORZO PASTA

1 Heat the butter and oil in a large skillet, add the chile, garlic, scallions, and zucchini, and cook over medium-low heat for 10-15 minutes, stirring frequently, until softened.

2 Reduce the heat and add the lemon zest. Cook gently for 3-4 minutes, add the cream cheese, and mix thoroughly. Season to taste.

3 Meanwhile, cook the pasta in a large saucepan of lightly salted boiling water according to the package directions until just tender.

4 Drain the pasta and add to the zucchini mixture. Stir in the parsley, mix well, and serve immediately.

1 tablespoon butter
1 tablespoon olive oil
1 red chile, seeded and finely chopped
2 garlic cloves, finely chopped
4 scallions, very finely chopped
3 zucchini, coarsely grated
finely grated zest of 1 small lemon
2/3 cup cream cheese with garlic and herbs
12 oz dried orzo (rice-shape pasta)
1/4 cup finely chopped flat leaf parsley
salt and black pepper

Serves **4**
Prep time **10 minutes**
Cooking time **15-20 minutes**

KALE & PESTO
Linguine

12 oz dried linguine
2 tablespoons olive oil
3 garlic cloves, crushed
4½ cups coarsely chopped, trimmed kale
⅔ cup toasted pine nuts
½ cup mascarpone cheese
1 cup grated vegetarian Pecorino-style cheese, plus extra shavings to garnish
½ teaspoon grated nutmeg
salt and black pepper

Serves **4**
Prep time **10 minutes**
Cooking time **10-12 minutes**

1 Cook the pasta in a large saucepan of lightly salted boiling water according to the package directions until just tender.

2 Meanwhile, heat the oil in a skillet, add the garlic, and sauté for 2-3 minutes. Add the kale to the pan. Cover with a lid and cook for 2-3 minutes or until the kale starts to wilt.

3 Using an immersion blender, or a food processor or blender if you have one, blend the pine nuts until smooth. Add the mascarpone, Pecorino, and nutmeg. Blend again. Add the kale and garlic mixture and blend until smooth. (If using an immersion blender, you may need to do this in batches.) Season to taste.

4 Drain the pasta and return it to the pan. Add the pesto and toss to mix well. Serve with shavings of cheese.

AFFORDABILITY 2

SPAGHETTI
WITH GARLIC & BLACK PEPPER

8 oz quick-cooking spaghetti
3 tablespoons olive oil
2 garlic cloves, chopped
2 tablespoons lemon juice
black pepper
grated vegetarian Parmesan-
  style cheese, to serve

Serves **2**
Prep time **5 minutes**
Cooking time **3-5 minutes**

1 Cook the spaghetti in a large saucepan of lightly salted boiling water for 3-5 minutes, or according to the package directions, until just tender.

2 Meanwhile, heat the oil in a skillet with the garlic and warm gently for 2-3 minutes, until softened but not browned.

3 Drain the spaghetti and return to the pan, reserving 3 tablespoons of the cooking water. Pour the garlic oil over the pasta and stir in the reserved cooking liquid and lemon juice. Season with black pepper and serve with grated cheese.

AFFORDABILITY 1

PACKING A
Lunch Punch

One quick and easy way to stretch your weekly budget is to take your own lunch and snacks into college. While late nights and lazy lie-ins mean it's tempting to grab breakfast or lunch from the cafeteria, every egg muffin and pot pie is eating into cash reserves that could be better spent on other things.

SMART CONTAINERS

There's nothing worse than unwrapping a soggy sandwich at lunchtime, so it's worth investing in a couple of decent containers. If you're planning to get more creative than encasing a wedge of cheese between two slices of white bread, you can find plenty of clever containers with compartments, folding cutlery, and separate sections for wet and dry ingredients. You might also want to buy a food thermos for hot meals and an insulated lunch bag to keep food cool in the summer. Get into the habit of emptying and cleaning your lunch container as soon as you get home; you will be more inspired to make a packed lunch again the next day if you don't have to face smelly food scraps first thing in the morning.

SNACK ATTACK

It's not just cafeteria meals that can break the budget; coffees and midmorning snacks all add up, too. It's a good idea to slip some fruit, nuts, granola bars, or homemade cookies into your bag for a quick energy boost during the day.

10 EASY LUNCH BOX IDEAS

1. Couscous salad—soak a handful of couscous in hot water for 15 minutes, then add chopped cucumber, red bell pepper, onion, celery, and herbs, and some drained chickpeas or kidney beans.

2. Fill a pita or wrap with shredded carrot, cheese, and hummus.

3. Treat yourself to a food thermos and enjoy a hot meal of soup or leftover pasta.

4. Fill a sealable plastic container with sliced carrots, celery, and cucumber and add a mini container of hummus.

5. Put layers of plain yogurt, muesli, chopped fruit, and honey into a sealable plastic container—don't forget a spoon.

6. Cold, cooked new potatoes make a great snack between lectures.

7. Cooked and cooled pasta can be mixed with pesto, cherry tomatoes, and chopped cucumber for a filling lunch.

8. Add a quartered boiled egg to a mixed green salad for a protein hit.

9. Make a hearty potato and vegetable frittata for dinner and enjoy the leftovers for lunch the next day.

10. Put your favorite filling between two slices of bread and enjoy a good, old-fashioned sandwich.

FLASH-IN-THE-PAN
Ratatouille

½ cup olive oil
2 onions, chopped
1 eggplant, cut into ¾ inch
cubes
2 large zucchini, cut into
¾ inch cubes
1 red bell pepper, cored, seeded,
and cut into ¾ inch pieces
1 yellow bell pepper, cored,
seeded, and cut into ¾ inch
pieces
2 garlic cloves, crushed
1 (14½ oz) can diced tomatoes
2-3 tablespoons balsamic
vinegar
1 teaspoon packed brown sugar
10-12 pitted black ripe olives
salt and black pepper
torn basil leaves, to garnish

Serves **4**
Prep time **10 minutes**
Cooking time **20 minutes**

1 Heat the oil in a large saucepan until hot, add all of the vegetables except the tomatoes, and stir-fry for a few minutes.

2 Add the tomatoes, balsamic vinegar, and sugar, season, and stir well. Cover with a tight-fitting lid and simmer for 15 minutes, until the vegetables are cooked.

3 Remove from the heat, sprinkle with the olives and torn basil leaves, and serve.

MIXED BEAN
KEDGEREE

1 Put the eggs into a saucepan of cold water and bring to a boil. Cook for 10 minutes, then plunge into cold water to cool. Shell the eggs, cut into wedges, and set aside.

2 Meanwhile, heat the oil in a saucepan, add the onion, and sauté for 3-4 minutes, until soft. Stir in the curry powder and rice, then add the broth. Bring to a boil, cover with a lid, and simmer for 10-15 minutes, until the rice is cooked.

3 Stir through the beans and sour cream. Season to taste, top with the eggs, and serve garnished with the tomatoes and herbs.

4 eggs
2 tablespoons vegetable oil
1 onion, chopped
2 tablespoons mild curry powder
1⅓ cups long grain rice
3 cups Vegetable Broth (see page 246)
4 cups rinsed, drained mixed beans, such as kidney, beans, pinto beans, and chickpeas
⅔ cup sour cream
salt and black pepper

To garnish
2 tomatoes, finely chopped
3 tablespoons chopped fresh herbs

Serves **4**
Prep time **10 minutes**
Cooking time **15-20 minutes**

AFFORDABILITY
1

GARLIC & PAPRIKA SOUP
WITH A FLOATING EGG

¼ cup olive oil
12 thick slices of baguette
5 garlic cloves, sliced
1 onion, finely chopped
1 tablespoon paprika
1 teaspoon ground cumin
good pinch of saffron
  threads
5 cups Vegetable Broth
  (see page 246)
1 oz dried soup pasta
4 eggs
salt and black pepper

Serves 4
Prep time **5 minutes**
Cooking time **20 minutes**

1 Heat the oil in a heavy saucepan, add the bread, and cook gently, turning once, until golden. Drain on paper towels.

2 Add the garlic, onion, paprika, and cumin to the pan and sauté gently for 3 minutes. Add the saffron and broth and bring to a boil. Stir in the soup pasta. Reduce the heat, cover with a lid, and simmer for about 8 minutes, until the pasta is just tender. Season to taste with salt and black pepper.

3 Break the eggs into a saucer and slide into the pan one at a time. Cook for about 2 minutes, until poached.

4 Stack three fried bread slices in each soup bowl. Ladle the soup over the bread, making sure each serving contains an egg. Serve immediately.

AFFORDABILITY
1

Eggplant PÂTÉ (V)

AFFORDABILITY
1

JUST A FEW DRIED MUSHROOMS REALLY BOOST THE FLAVOR OF THIS QUICK-AND-EASY PÂTÉ. IT MAKES PLENTY, AND LEFTOVERS KEEP WELL IN THE REFRIGERATOR FOR SEVERAL DAYS, READY FOR EITHER ZIPPING UP VEGETABLE STEWS OR SPREADING ONTO TOAST AND BROILING TOPPED WITH SWISS CHEESE.

1 oz dried porcini mushrooms
1 eggplant
⅓ cup olive oil
1 small red onion, chopped
2 teaspoons cumin seeds
6 oz white or cremini
   mushrooms
2 garlic cloves, crushed
3 pickled walnuts, halved
small handful of fresh cilantro
salt and black pepper
toasted walnut or whole-grain
   bread, to serve

Serves 6
Prep time **10 minutes,
plus soaking**
Cooking time **15 minutes**

1 Put the dried mushrooms into a bowl and cover with plenty of boiling water. Let soak for 10 minutes.

2 Meanwhile, cut the eggplant into ½ inch dice. Heat the oil in a large skillet, add the eggplant and onion, and sauté gently for 8 minutes, until the vegetables are softened and browned.

3 Drain the dried mushrooms and add to the pan with the cumin seeds, fresh mushrooms, and garlic. Sauté for another 5-7 minutes, until the eggplant is soft.

4 Transfer to a food processor or blender with the pickled walnuts and cilantro, season to taste with salt and black pepper, and process until broken up but not completely smooth. Alternatively, blend the ingredients in a bowl using an immersion blender. Transfer to a serving dish and serve warm or cold with toast.

All the Carbs

ZUCCHINI & CREAMY TOMATO PENNE

SWISS CHEESE MELTS

SPINACH & POTATO GRATIN

GOAT CHEESE & PEPPER
LASAGNE

2 oz dried porcini mushrooms
7½ cups trimmed spinach
¼ cup olive oil
1 large onion, sliced
2 red bell peppers, cored,
  seeded, and coarsely chopped
3 garlic cloves, sliced
2 (14½ oz) cans diced tomatoes
¼ cup homemade (see
  page 249) or store-bought
  red pesto
2 tablespoons chopped oregano
10 oz soft goat cheese
2 quantities White Sauce
  (see page 247)
8 oz dried lasagna noodles
1 cup fresh bread crumbs
salt and black pepper

Serves 4-5
Prep time **30 minutes,
plus soaking**
Cooking time **1 hour**

1 Put the mushrooms in a bowl, cover with 1 cup of boiling water, and let soak. Steam the spinach for 1-2 minutes, until just wilted.

2 Heat 2 tablespoons of the oil in a saucepan, add the onion and bell peppers, and sauté for 5 minutes. Add the garlic, tomatoes, pesto, oregano, spinach, mushrooms and their soaking liquid, and salt and black pepper. Bring to a boil and simmer gently for 10 minutes.

3 Beat the goat cheese into the white sauce. Spoon one-quarter of the vegetable sauce into a shallow, 1½ quart ovenproof dish. Spread with one-quarter of the white sauce. Arrange one-third of the pasta noodles over the sauce, trimming or breaking them to fit.

4 Repeat the layering, finishing with white sauce. Toss the bread crumbs with the remaining oil and sprinkle them over the sauce. Bake in a preheated oven, at 375ºF, for 45 minutes or until golden.

AFFORDABILITY 3

ZUCCHINI & MASCARPONE
Lasagne

1 Put the dried mushrooms in a bowl, cover with boiling water, and let soak. Bring a large saucepan of water to a boil with 1 tablespoon of the oil. Add the pasta noodles, one at a time, and cook for about 4 minutes, until just tender. Drain.

2 Meanwhile, mix together the mascarpone, garlic, and dill or tarragon in a small bowl and season to taste with salt and black pepper. Melt half the butter in a skillet, add the bread crumbs, and sauté gently for 2 minutes. Drain on paper towels.

3 Melt the remaining butter in the pan with the remaining oil. Add the fresh mushrooms and zucchini and sauté for about 6 minutes, until golden. Drain the dried mushrooms, add to the pan, and cook for 1 minute.

4 Lay four pieces of lasagna noodles, spaced slightly apart, in a shallow ovenproof dish. Spoon one-third of the vegetables over them, then a spoonful of the mascarpone mixture. Add another piece of lasagna noodle to each stack and spoon more vegetables and mascarpone over it. Finally, add the remaining lasagna noodles, vegetables, and mascarpone.

5 Sprinkle with the fried bread crumbs and bake in a preheated oven, at 400°F, for 6–8 minutes, until heated through.

1 oz dried porcini mushrooms
3 tablespoons olive oil
4 oz fresh lasagna noodles, halved
1 cup mascarpone cheese
2 garlic cloves, crushed
3 tablespoons chopped dill or tarragon
2 tablespoons butter
1 cup fresh bread crumbs
1 (16 oz) package white mushrooms, sliced (8 cups)
2 zucchini, sliced
salt and black pepper

Serves 4
Prep time **15 minutes, plus soaking**
Cooking time **20 minutes**

AFFORDABILITY 2

VEGGIE
CARBONARA

12 oz dried penne
2 tablespoons olive oil
2 garlic cloves, finely chopped
3 zucchini, thinly sliced
6 scallions, cut into ¼ inch
  lengths
4 egg yolks
½ crème fraîche or cream
  cheese
¾ cup grated vegetarian
  Parmesan-style cheese,
  plus extra to serve
salt and black pepper

Serves **4**
Prep time **5 minutes**
Cooking time **10-12 minutes**

1 Cook the pasta in a large saucepan of lightly salted boiling water according to the package directions until just tender.

2 Meanwhile, heat the oil in a heavy skillet over medium-high heat, add the garlic, zucchini, and scallions, and cook, stirring, for 4-5 minutes or until the zucchini are tender. Remove the pan from the heat and set aside.

3 Put the egg yolks in a bowl and season with salt and a generous grinding of black pepper. Mix together with a fork.

4 Just before the pasta is ready, return the pan with the zucchini mixture to the heat. Stir in the crème fraîche or cream cheese and bring to a boil.

5 Drain the pasta well, return to the pan, and immediately stir in the egg mixture, cheese, and the creamy zucchini mixture. Stir vigorously and serve immediately with a sprinkling of extra grated cheese.

AFFORDABILITY **1**

Haloumi & ARUGULA CARBONARA

1 Cook the pasta in a saucepan of lightly salted boiling water for about 10 minutes, or according to the package directions, until just tender.

2 Meanwhile, beat together the egg yolk, egg, cream, garlic, and a little salt and black pepper in a small bowl. Heat the oil in a skillet and cook the haloumi or Muenster for 2–3 minutes, stirring occasionally until golden.

3 Drain the pasta and return to the saucepan. Add the haloumi and the egg mixture and stir together, adding the arugula once the pasta is coated in the sauce. Keep stirring the ingredients together until the arugula has wilted slightly and the eggs have thickened in the heat of the pasta. Sprinkle with parsley and serve immediately.

4 oz dried spaghetti or linguine
1 egg yolk
1 egg
⅓ cup light cream
1 garlic clove, crushed
2 teaspoons olive oil
3 oz haloumi or Muenster cheese, cut into small dice
2 cups arugula
salt and black pepper
chopped parsley, to garnish

Serves 1
Prep time **5 minutes**
Cooking time **12–15 minutes**

AFFORDABILITY
2

EGGPLANT CANNELLONI

4 large fresh or dried lasagna
  noodles
2 eggplants, thinly sliced
4 tablespoons olive oil
1 teaspoon finely chopped
  thyme
1 cup ricotta cheese
2/3 cup basil leaves, torn
  into pieces
2 garlic cloves, crushed
1 quantity Tomato Sauce
  (see page 247)
1 cup shredded fontina,
  Gruyère, or Swiss cheese
salt and black pepper

Serves 4
Prep time **30 minutes**
Cooking time **50 minutes**

1 Bring a saucepan of salted water to a boil. Add the lasagna noodles, return to a boil, and cook, allowing 2 minutes for fresh and 8–10 minutes for dried, or according to the pacage directions. Drain the noodles and immerse in cold water.

2 Place the eggplants in a single layer on a foil-lined broiler rack. (You may need to do this in batches.) Mix the olive oil, thyme, and salt and black pepper and brush over the eggplants. Broil until lightly browned, turning once.

3 Beat the ricotta with the basil, garlic, and a little salt and black pepper. Thoroughly drain the pasta noodles and lay them on the work surface. Cut each in half. Spread the ricotta mixture over the noodles, right to the edges. Arrange the eggplant slices on top. Roll up each piece.

4 Spread two-thirds of the tomato sauce in a shallow ovenproof dish and arrange the cannelloni on top. Spoon over the remaining tomato sauce and sprinkle with the cheese. Bake in a preheated oven, at 375°F, for 20 minutes or until the cheese is golden.

AFFORDABILITY 2

MUSHROOM TAGLIATELLE with *Gremolata*

½ oz dried porcini mushrooms
4 tablespoons butter
¼ cup olive oil
1 small onion, finely chopped
3 cups thinly sliced cremini or
  white mushrooms
¼ cup chopped herbs, such
  as parsley, tarragon, fennel,
  or basil
finely grated zest of 1 lemon
2 garlic cloves, finely chopped
1 lb fresh tagliatelle
salt and black pepper

Serves 4
Prep time **15 minutes,
plus soaking**
Cooking time **10 minutes**

1 Put the porcini mushrooms into a bowl, cover with boiling water, and let soak for 15 minutes.

2 Melt the butter with 1 tablespoon of the oil in a skillet, add the onion, and sauté for 4 minutes, until softened. Drain the soaked mushrooms. Thinly slice the porcini mushrooms and add them to the pan with the cremini or white mushrooms and one-quarter of the herbs. Sauté gently for 5 minutes.

3 Meanwhile, cook the pasta in a large saucepan of lightly salted boiling water for about 3 minutes, or according to the package directions, until just tender.

4 Make the gremolata. Mix the remaining herbs with the lemon zest, garlic, and plenty of black pepper.

5 Drain the pasta and return to the saucepan. Add the mushroom mixture and toss the ingredients with the remaining oil. Serve with the gremolata.

AFFORDABILITY 1

ZUCCHINI & CREAMY TOMATO PENNE

12 oz dried penne
1 tablespoon olive oil
1 onion, chopped
1 garlic clove, finely chopped
3 zucchini, chopped
1 red bell pepper, cored,
    seeded, and chopped
1 cup mascarpone cheese
1 cup tomato puree or sauce
salt and black pepper
2 tablespoons chopped basil,
    plus extra to garnish

Serves 4
Prep time 10 minutes
Cooking time 15 minutes

1 Cook the pasta in a large saucepan of lightly salted boiling water according to the package directions until just tender.

2 Meanwhile, heat the oil in a skillet, add the onion and garlic, and sauté over medium heat for 3 minutes, until softened. Stir in the zucchini and red bell pepper and cook for 5 minutes, until the zucchini have softened.

3 Stir the mascarpone into the pan until melted, then add the tomato puree or sauce and simmer for 2-3 minutes. Season to taste with salt and black pepper and stir in the basil.

4 Drain the pasta and return to the pan. Stir the sauce into the cooked pasta and toss well. Serve immediately with the basil sprinkled over the top.

AFFORDABILITY 1

TAGLIATELLE
with Blue Cheese Butter

½ cup crumbled Stilton or other
    creamy blue cheese
2 tablespoons butter, softened
pinch of grated nutmeg
4 oz dried tagliatelle
2 cups bite-size broccoli pieces
salt and black pepper

Serves 1
Prep time **5 minutes**
Cooking time **10 minutes**

1 Mash the cheese in a bowl with a fork to break it up. Add the butter, nutmeg, and a little pepper and beat well to mix.

2 Cook the pasta in a large saucepan of lightly salted boiling water according to the package directions until tender. About 3 minutes before the final cooking time, add the broccoli stems and cook for 2 minutes, then add the florets and cook for another 1 minute, until the pasta and broccoli are tender.

3 Drain the pasta and broccoli and return to the pan. Dot half the cheese butter into the pan so it melts over the hot pasta. Dot the remaining butter into the pasta and serve immediately.

CREAMY MUSHROOM & TARRAGON RIGATONI

4 tablespoons butter
1 tablespoon vegetable oil
1 large leek, trimmed and thinly
   sliced
1 garlic clove, chopped
2 cups sliced mushrooms
1 teaspoon dried tarragon
½ cup Vegetable Broth
   (see page 246)
1 cup light cream
12 oz dried rigatoni or
   tortiglioni pasta
salt and black pepper
4 teaspoons grated vegetarian
   Parmesan-style cheese,
   to serve

Serves **4**
Prep time **5 minutes**
Cooking time **15 minutes**

1 Heat the butter and oil in a large nonstick skillet until the butter is frothing. Add the leek and garlic and sauté for 2-3 minutes, until beginning to soften. Add the mushrooms and tarragon and cook for another 4-5 minutes, until soft and golden.

2 Pour the vegetable broth and cream into the mushrooms, then season generously with salt and black pepper. Simmer gently for 6-7 minutes.

3 Meanwhile, cook the pasta in a large saucepan of lightly salted boiling water for 11 minutes, or according to the package directions, until just tender.

4 Drain the pasta and stir into the sauce. Serve immediately, sprinkled with grated cheese.

AFFORDABILITY
1

RIBBON PASTA
WITH EGGPLANTS & PINE NUTS

½ cup olive oil
2 eggplants, diced
2 red onions, sliced
½ cup pine nuts
3 garlic cloves, crushed
⅓ cup tomato paste
⅔ cup Vegetable Broth
  (see page 246)
12 oz fresh ribbon pasta
1 cup pitted black ripe olives
salt and black pepper
3 tablespoons coarsely chopped
  flat leaf parsley, to garnish

1 Heat the oil in a large skillet, add the eggplants and onions, and sauté for 8-10 minutes, until golden and tender. Add the pine nuts and garlic and sauté for 2 minutes. Stir in the tomato paste and broth and cook for 2 minutes.

2 Meanwhile, cook the pasta in a large saucepan of lightly salted boiling water for about 2 minutes, or according to the package directions, until just tender.

3 Drain the pasta and return to the pan. Add the sauce and olives, season to taste with salt and black pepper, and toss together over medium heat for 1 minute until combined. Sprinkle with parsley and serve immediately.

Serves **4**
Prep time **5 minutes**
Cooking time **15 minutes**

GOAT CHEESE LINGUINE
WITH GARLIC & HERB BUTTER

1 Thickly slice the goat cheese and arrange on a lightly oiled, aluminum foil-lined broiler rack. Broil under a preheated hot broiler for about 2 minutes, until golden. Keep warm.

2 Using a zester, pare zest strips from the lemon, then squeeze the juice.

3 Heat the butter and oil in a skillet, add the shallots and garlic, and sauté gently for 3 minutes. Stir in the herbs, capers, and lemon juice, and season to taste with salt and black pepper.

4 Meanwhile, cook the pasta in a saucepan of lightly salted boiling water for about 2 minutes, or according to the package directions, until just tender. Drain lightly and return to the saucepan. Add the goat cheese and herb butter sauce and toss the ingredients together gently. Serve sprinkled with strips of lemon zest.

10 oz firm goat cheese
1 lemon
2 tablespoons olive oil, plus
    extra for oiling
6 tablespoons butter
3 shallots, finely chopped
2 garlic cloves, crushed
½ cup mixed chopped herbs,
    such as tarragon, chervil,
    parsley, and dill
3 tablespoons capers, drained
12 oz fresh linguine
salt and black pepper

Serves **4**
Prep time **5 minutes**
Cooking time **7 minutes**

AFFORDABILITY
3

PASTA
WITH FENNEL & ARUGULA

1 tablespoon olive oil
1 fennel bulb, trimmed and
  thinly sliced
1 garlic clove, chopped
½ cup Vegetable Broth
  (see page 246)
¼ cup crème fraîche or cream
  cheese
grated zest and juice of 1 small
  lemon
2 cups arugula
8 oz fresh tagliatelle or
  pappardelle
salt and black pepper
grated vegetarian Parmesan-
  style cheese, to serve

Serves **2**
Prep time **10 minutes**
Cooking time **15 minutes**

1 Heat the oil in a skillet, add the fennel and garlic, and cook gently for about 10 minutes, until the fennel is soft and golden.

2 Add the broth to the pan and cook until reduced by half. Stir in the crème fraîche or cream cheese, lemon zest and juice, and arugula and cook, stirring, until the arugula has wilted. Season to taste with salt and black pepper.

3 Meanwhile, cook the pasta in a large saucepan of lightly salted boiling water for 3-4 minutes, or according to the pack directions, until just tender. Drain and return to the pan.

4 Stir the sauce into the cooked pasta and toss well. Season with freshly ground black pepper and serve immediately with the cheese.

MACARONI & CHEESE
WITH SPINACH

12 oz dried macaroni
4 tablespoons butter
⅓ cup all-purpose flour
3 cups milk
1½ cups chopped Taleggio,
  fontina, or American
  cheese
2 teaspoons whole-grain
  mustard
1 teaspoon Dijon mustard
1 (12 oz) package baby
  spinach
8 cherry tomatoes, halved
1 cup fresh white bread
  crumbs
¼ cup shredded cheddar
  or American cheese
salt and black pepper

Serves 4
Prep time 10 minutes
Cooking time 30 minutes

1 Cook the macaroni in a large saucepan of lightly salted boiling water for 8-10 minutes, or according to the package directions, until just tender.

2 Meanwhile, put the butter, flour, and milk into a saucepan and whisk constantly over medium heat until the sauce boils and thickens. Simmer for 2-3 minutes, until you have a smooth glossy sauce, then reduce the heat to low and stir in the chopped cheese and mustards. Season to taste with salt and black pepper and cook gently until the cheese has melted.

3 Add the spinach to the pasta pan and cook for another 1 minute, until wilted. Drain well and place in a 1½ quart ovenproof dish.

4 Pour the sauce over the macaroni and spinach, spread the tomatoes over them, and then sprinkle with the bread crumbs and shredded cheese. Bake in a preheated oven, at 400°F, for 20 minutes, until golden and bubbling.

AFFORDABILITY 1

MUSHROOM & EGG
ALL-DAY PIZZA

1 Preheat oven to 475°F. Put the flour, yeast, sugar, and salt into a mixing bowl and add the warm milk and water mixture and 2 tablespoons of the oill. Mix together with a blunt knife to form a soft dough.

2 Turn out the dough onto a floured surface and knead for 10 minutes, until the dough is smooth and elastic. Put into a lightly oiled bowl, cover with plastic wrap, and let rise in a warm place for about 45 minutes, until risen to twice the size.

3 Mix the remaining oil with the garlic and a little salt and black pepper. Turn out the dough onto a floured surface and cut in half. Roll out each piece until about 9 inches in diameter and transfer to baking sheets.

4 Sprinkle the mushrooms over one side of each pizza. Brush the garlic oil over the pizzas and mushroom slices and let stand for 10 minutes.

5 Carefully break 2 eggs onto each pizza, season with black pepper, and bake for 12 minutes, until both pizza crusts and eggs are cooked through. Serve sprinkled with sprouts, if desired.

1¼ cups white bread flour, plus extra for dusting
1 teaspoon active dry yeast
½ teaspoon sugar
½ teaspoon salt
½ cup mixed milk and water, lukewarm
3 tablespoons olive oil, plus extra for greasing
1 garlic clove, crushed
2 large portobello mushrooms, sliced
4 eggs
alfalfa sprouts (optional), to serve
salt and black pepper

....
Serves **2**
Prep time **25 minutes, plus standing and proving**
Cooking time **12 minutes**
....

SWISS CHEESE MELTS

1 large French baguette
2 cups shredded Swiss cheese
1 tablespoon whole-grain mustard
2 tablespoons mayonnaise
2 tomatoes, seeded and chopped
pinch of black pepper
1 round lettuce, to serve (optional)

Serves 4
Prep time 10 minutes
Cooking time 3-4 minutes

1 Cut the French baguette in half, then slice each half horizontally to form four long pieces. Put the shredded cheese into a bowl with the remaining ingredients and mix well to combine.

2 Spoon the topping over the cut side of each piece of bread and place on a baking sheet. Cook under a preheated hot broiler for 3-4 minutes, until golden and bubbling. Serve hot with lettuce leaves, if desired.

STUDENT TIP

Give dirty pans and plates a quick rinse when you've finished using them. If you can't face washing them after dinner, the water will loosen the worst of the food and you won't have to spend ages scrubbing off dried chunks the next morning. Better still, soak them in soapy water.

SPICY MEXICAN WRAPS

1 Heat the oil in a saucepan, add the onion, and sauté for 5 minutes, until softened. Stir in the garlic and spices and cook for another 1 minute.

2 Add the beans, tomatoes, ketchup, and a little salt and bring to a boil. Reduce the heat to its lowest setting and cook gently for 15-20 minutes, until thick and pulpy.

3 Meanwhile, halve the avocado and discard the pit. Peel away the skin and thinly slice the flesh.

4 Heat a dry skillet and warm the tortillas through briefly. Spread each wrap with a layer of bean mixture, sprinkle with cheese and avocado slices, and dot with sour cream. Roll up to enclose the filling and serve.

2 tablespoons vegetable oil
1 onion, chopped
1 garlic clove, finely chopped
½ teaspoon ground coriander
½ teaspoon ground cumin
1 teaspoon mild chili powder
1 (15 oz) can red kidney beans, rinsed and drained
1 (14½ oz) can diced tomatoes
2 tablespoons ketchup
1 avocado
4 seeded tortilla wraps
¾ cup shredded cheddar cheese
¼ cup sour cream
salt

Serves **4**
Prep time **15 minutes**
Cooking time **25-30 minutes**

AFFORDABILITY
1

TORTILLAS
with Minted Chile
& EGGPLANT YOGURT

¼ cup olive oil
1 eggplant, thinly sliced
small handful of mint, chopped
small handful of parsley, chopped
2 tablespoons chopped chives
1 green chile, seeded and thinly sliced
1 cup Greek yogurt
2 tablespoons mayonnaise
2 large tortillas
3 inch length of cucumber, thinly sliced
salt and black pepper
paprika, to garnish

Serves **2**
Prep time **10 minutes, plus cooling**
Cooking time **10 minutes**

1 Heat the oil in a skillet, add the eggplant, and sauté for about 10 minutes, until golden. Drain and let cool.

2 Mix the herbs with the chile, yogurt, and mayonnaise in a bowl and season to taste with salt and black pepper.

3 Arrange the fried eggplant slices over the tortillas and spread with the Greek yogurt mixture. Arrange the cucumber slices on top. Roll up each tortilla, sprinkle with paprika, and serve.

Camembert WRAPS WITH HOT PEPPER SALSA

2 tablespoons vegetable oil
1 red onion, chopped
2 celery sticks, chopped
2 red bell peppers, cored,
  seeded, and chopped
1 yellow bell pepper, cored,
  seeded, and chopped
¼ cup chopped fresh cilantro
2 teaspoons white wine vinegar
2 teaspoons honey
8 oz round Camembert cheese
4 tortilla wraps
2 cups pea shoots or mixed
  salad greens
salt and black pepper

Serves **4**
Prep time **20 minutes**
Cooking time **25 minutes**

1 Heat the oil in a skillet, add the onion, celery, and bell peppers, and sauté gently for 15 minutes or until softened and lightly browned. Stir in the cilantro, vinegar, and honey and season to taste.

2 Place the camembert on a board and slice horizontally into 4 thin circles. Place a round on top of each tortilla and position two of them on separate baking sheets. Cook in a preheated oven, at 400°F, for 3-4 minutes, until the cheese has softened. Remove from the oven and cook the remaining two in the same way.

3 Spread the softened cheese toward the edges of the tortillas with the back of a spoon. Spread the bell pepper mixture on top and sprinkle with the greens. Roll up the tortillas and serve.

AFFORDABILITY 1

RICE PILAF
with Kale Chips

2 tablespoons vegetable oil
1 red onion, chopped
3 garlic cloves, crushed
1 cup red rice, rinsed
2 cups Vegetable Broth
  (see page 246)
1 cinnamon stick (optional)
8 cardamom pods, crushed
  to expose the seeds
1 peach or nectarine, halved,
  pitted, and diced
3 tablespoons chopped mint
½ cup chopped nuts, such
  as almonds, hazelnuts, or
  walnuts

Kale chips
4 oz kale
1 tablespoon olive oil
salt and black pepper

Serves **2**
Prep time **20 minutes**
Cooking time **50 minutes**

1 Heat the vegetable oil in a saucepan, add the onion, and gently sauté for 5 minutes. Add the garlic and rice and cook for another 2 minutes. Pour in the broth and bring to a gentle simmer. Add the cinnamon, if using, and cardamom, cover with a lid, and cook gently for 40 minutes, until the rice is tender and the broth is absorbed.

2 Meanwhile, thoroughly wash and dry the kale (a salad spinner is ideal, but you can also pat it dry between layers of paper towels). Tear into pieces if the kale hasn't already been prepared, discarding any thick stems. Drizzle the oil over the kale with a little salt and black pepper. Mix well.

3 Turn out onto a baking sheet and bake in a preheated oven, at 350°F, for 10 minutes, until crisp. Be careful to avoid overcooking the kale or it'll turn bitter.

4 Stir the peach or nectarine, mint, and nuts into the rice. Season to taste and transfer to warm serving plates. Sprinkle the kale on top and serve.

Creamy Mushroom & Chive Risotto

4 tablespoons butter
1 onion, finely chopped
2 garlic cloves, finely chopped
5 cups chopped mushrooms,
   preferably brown button
2 cups risotto rice
5½ cups hot Vegetable Broth
   (see page 246)
3 tablespoons crème fraîche
   or sour cream
2 tablespoons chopped chives
salt and black pepper
grated vegetarian Parmesan-
   style cheese, to serve
   (optional)

Serves **4**
Prep time **10 minutes**
Cooking time **30 minutes**

1 Melt the butter in a saucepan, add the onion and garlic, and sauté over medium heat for 4–5 minutes. Add the mushrooms and cook for 2–3 minutes, stirring occasionally. Add the risotto rice and cook, stirring, for 1 minute.

2 Add a small ladleful of hot broth and cook, stirring frequently, until almost absorbed. Add a little more broth and continue cooking, stirring frequently, until almost absorbed. Continue in the same way until all the broth is used and the rice is creamy but still retaining a little bite. This will take about 20 minutes.

3 Stir the crème fraîche or sour cream and chives into the risotto and season well. Remove from the heat, cover with a lid, and let stand for 2 minutes. Serve sprinkled with grated cheese.

AFFORDABILITY
1

EASY PEA RISOTTO

AFFORDABILITY
1

1 Melt the butter in a flameproof casserole, add the onion, and sauté for 5 minutes, until softened. Add the garlic and rice and cook, stirring, for 1 minute, until coated in the butter. Stir in the broth and bring to a boil. (If you don't have a flameproof casserole, cook the ingredients in a saucepan and transfer to a baking dish.)

2 Cover with a lid or aluminum foil and bake in a preheated oven, at 350°F, for 15 minutes. Stir in the peas, chives, and dill and return to the oven for another 10 minutes, until the peas are cooked through. If the risotto has dried out, stir in a splash of water.

3 Season to taste and serve sprinkled with plenty of grated cheese.

2 tablespoons butter
1 onion, finely chopped
1 garlic clove, crushed
1 cup risotto rice
2 cups hot Vegetable Broth
  (see page 246)
1 cup frozen peas
¼ cup chopped chives
2 tablespoons chopped dill
salt and black pepper
grated vegetarian Parmesan-
  style cheese, to serve

Serves **2**
Prep time **10 minutes**
Cooking time **40 minutes**

STUDENT TIP

If you're used to the luxury of brand-name foods, it might be a shock to the system to fill up your basket with store-brand equivalents. However, these days a lot of supermarket own-label foods are indistinguishable from their big-brand counterparts and your weekly shopping will be a lot cheaper.

BEET RISOTTO
with Horseradish
& MIXED GREENS

IF YOU CAN FIND FRESH HORSERADISH, USE IT IN PLACE OF THE STORE-BOUGHT PREPARED TYPE. THE FLAVOR IS FAR SUPERIOR, BUT BEWARE OF ITS HEAT INTENSITY, WHICH CAN BE ANYTHING FROM HARMLESSLY MILD TO HOT AND FIERCE, DEPENDING ON ITS FRESHNESS.

¼ cup olive oil
1 large red onion, chopped
3 garlic cloves, crushed
2 cups risotto rice
5½ cups hot Vegetable Broth (see page 246)
3 cups finely diced cooked beets
¼ cup coarsely chopped dill
1–2 tablespoons freshly grated horseradish or 1 tablespoon hot horseradish from a jar
½ cup salted macadamia nuts or almonds
salt and black pepper
mixed salad greens, to serve

Serves **4**
Prep time **5 minutes**
Cooking time **25 minutes**

1 Heat the oil in a large, heavy saucepan, add the onion and garlic, and sauté gently for 3 minutes. Add the rice and cook, stirring, for 1 minute.

2 Add 2 ladlefuls of the broth and cook, stirring frequently, until almost absorbed. Add a little more broth and continue cooking, stirring frequently, until almost absorbed. Continue in the same way until all the broth is used and the rice is creamy but still retaining a little bite. This will take about 20 minutes.

3 Stir in the beets, dill, horseradish, and nuts, season to taste, and heat through gently for 1 minute. Serve with mixed salad greens.

Lemon & Herb RISOTTO

1 Heat the oil in a heavy saucepan, add the shallots, garlic, celery, zucchini, and carrot, and sauté over low heat for 4 minutes or until the vegetables have softened. Add the rice, increase the heat, and cook, stirring, for 2–3 minutes.

2 Add a ladleful of hot broth, half the herbs, and season well. Cook, stirring frequently, until the broth is almost absorbed. Reduce the heat to medium-low, add a little more broth, and continue cooking, stirring constantly, until almost absorbed. Continue in the same way until all the broth is used and the rice is cooked through but still retaining a little bite. This will take about 20 minutes.

3 Remove from the heat and gently stir in the remaining herbs, butter, lemon zest, and cheese. Cover with a lid and let stand for 2–3 minutes, during which time it will become creamy and oozy. Serve immediately, sprinkled with freshly ground black pepper.

1 tablespoon olive oil
3 shallots, finely chopped
2 garlic cloves, finely chopped
½ head of celery, finely chopped
1 zucchini, finely diced
1 carrot, peeled and finely diced
1²⁄₃ cups risotto rice
5 cups hot Vegetable Broth (see page 246)
large handful of fresh mixed herbs, such as tarragon, parsley, chives, and dill
1 stick butter
1 tablespoon finely grated lemon zest
1 cup grated vegetarian Parmesan-style cheese
salt and black pepper

Serves **4**
Prep time **10 minutes**
Cooking time **30 minutes**

COOKING TIP

If you use a lot of fresh herbs in cooking, try growing your own. You don't need outside space—a windowsill will do—and hardy herbs, such as rosemary and thyme, can be used to liven up all kinds of dishes.

AFFORDABILITY
2

SAGE & TOMATO PILAF (V)

1 Cut each tomato into eight and thickly slice the bell pepper quarters. Put into a roasting pan with the onion, then drizzle with the oil and season well. Tear some of the sage into pieces and sprinkle over the vegetables. Roast in a preheated oven, at 400°F, for 40-45 minutes, until softened.

2 Meanwhile, cook the rice in a saucepan of boiling water for 15 minutes, or according to the package directions, until tender. Drain well.

3 Mix the rice into the cooked tomatoes and bell peppers, then sprinkle with the remaining sage leaves. Serve with warm bread.

8 plum tomatoes
1 red bell pepper, cored, seeded, and quartered
1 onion, coarsely chopped
2 tablespoons olive oil
1 small bunch of sage
1 cup quick-cooking long grain white and wild rice mix
salt and black pepper
warm ciabatta or herb bread, to serve

Serves **4**
Prep time **15 minutes**
Cooking time **40-45 minutes**

AFFORDABILITY 1

CARROT & FETA
Potato Cakes

1 Cook the carrots and potatoes in a large saucepan of lightly salted boiling water for about 12 minutes, until tender. Drain well and mash together until crushed but not completely smooth. Let cool, uncovered, for at least 10 minutes.

2 While the potatoes and carrots are cooling, add the beaten egg, feta, cumin, parsley, scallions, and a pinch each of salt and black pepper to the pan and mix well to combine. Use flour-dusted hands to shape the mixture into four patties.

3 Heat the oil in a large nonstick skillet and pan-fry the patties gently for about 3 minutes on each side until crisp and golden. Drain on paper towels and serve with fried or poached eggs, if desired.

2 medium or 1 large carrot, peeled and diced
3 russet or Yukon gold potatoes, peeled and diced
1 medium egg, lightly beaten
½ cup crumbled feta cheese
1 teaspoon ground cumin
1 tablespoon chopped parsley (optional)
2 scallions, chopped
flour, for dusting
3–4 tablespoons vegetable oil
salt and black pepper
2 poached or fried eggs, to serve (optional)

Serves **2**
Prep time **15 minutes,** **plus cooling**
Cooking time **20 minutes**

AFFORDABILITY
1

WARM MUSHROOMS WITH HASH BROWNS

1 Cook the potatoes whole in a large saucepan of lightly salted boiling water for 8-10 minutes. Drain and set aside to cool slightly. Coarsely grate the potatoes and mix in a bowl with the sliced onion, 2 tablespoons oil, and plenty of salt and black pepper.

2 Heat the remaining oil in a large nonstick skillet and add the potato mixture, pushing down to flatten it so that it covers the bottom of the pan. Cook for 7-8 minutes, then slide onto an oiled plate or board. Flip the hash brown back into the pan to cook the other side for 7-8 minutes, until crisp and golden.

3 Meanwhile, melt the butter in a skillet and cook the garlic and mushrooms gently for 6-7 minutes, until golden. Season to taste with salt and black pepper, then stir in the chopped parsley, if using. Cut the hash brown into wedges, then arrange on serving plates, sprinkle with the watercress and spoon over the warm mushrooms with their juices. Serve immediately.

4 russet or Yukon gold potatoes, scrubbed but unpeeled
½ onion, very thinly sliced
¼ cup vegetable oil
4 tablespoons butter
1 garlic clove, chopped
4 cups thinly sliced white mushrooms
2 tablespoons finely chopped parsley (optional)
salt and black pepper
1 large bunch of watercress or handful of arugula, to serve

Serves 4
Prep time **15 minutes**
Cooking time **20-25 minutes**

AFFORDABILITY
1

Chimichurri FRIES & BEANS

1 Scrub or peel the sweet potatoes and cut into chunky sticks. Sprinkle in a roasting pan with the red onions, drizzle with 1 tablespoon of the oil, and mix together. Bake in a preheated oven, at 400°F, for 25 minutes, until the potatoes are golden and just tender. Stir once or twice during cooking so the vegetables brown evenly.

2 Blend the cornstarch with 2 tablespoons of cold water in a small bowl. Add the lime zest and half the juice, the sugar, soy sauce, and lima beans. Stir well.

3 Pour the mixture over the potatoes, mix well, and return to the oven for 10 minutes, stirring the ingredients after 5 minutes so the juices thicken evenly.

4 Mix the remaining oil with the red pepper flakes, parsley, cilantro, scallions, and remaining lime juice. Spoon the vegetables and beans onto warm serving plates and drizzle with the sauce.

2 large sweet potatoes
2 red onions, cut into wedges
3 tablespoons vegetable oil
1 teaspoon cornstarch
finely grated zest and juice
   of 1 lime
2 teaspoons packed light brown
   or granulated sugar
2 tablespoons soy sauce
1 (15 oz) can lima beans, rinsed
   and drained
¼ teaspoon dried red
   pepper flakes
3 tablespoons chopped parsley
3 tablespoons chopped fresh
   cilantro
2 scallions, finely chopped

Serves 2
Prep time 15 minutes
Cooking time 55 minutes

Jamaican COCONUT CURRY

1 Heat the oil in a large skillet or saucepan, add the ginger, chile, ground spices, and onions, and sauté gently for about 5 minutes, stirring occasionally, until the onions have softened. Add the garlic and sauté for another 1 minute.

2 Add the potatoes to the pan with the broth and coconut milk. Bring to a gentle simmer, cover with a lid, and cook gently for 20-25 minutes, until the potatoes are tender.

3 Add the tomatoes, zucchini, and peas and cook for 15 minutes, until all the vegetables are tender and the juices are beginning to thicken. Season to taste and serve with lemon or lime wedges for squeezing over the curry.

¼ cup vegetable oil
½ cup peeled and grated fresh ginger root
1 red chile, seeded and finely chopped
2 teaspoons ground cumin
2 teaspoons ground coriander
1 teaspoon turmeric
2 onions, coarsely chopped
4 garlic cloves, crushed
1½ lb new potatoes, cut into ¾ inch chunks
1¼ cups Vegetable Broth (see page 246)
⅔ cup coconut milk
2 tomatoes, skinned and chopped
2 small zucchini, thinly sliced
⅔ cup peas
salt and black pepper
lemon or lime wedges, to serve

Serves 3-4
Prep time **25 minutes**
Cooking time **45-50 minutes**

VEGETABLE NOODLES
in Spiced Coconut Milk

A SINGLE THAI CHILE GIVES THIS DISH A REALLY FIERCE KICK. SUBSTITUTE A MILD CHILE IF YOU ARE FEELING CAUTIOUS.

1 Put the noodles into a bowl, cover with boiling water, and let stand while preparing the vegetables, or prepare according to the package directions.

2 Heat the oil in a large saucepan, add the onion, chile, garlic, ginger, coriander, turmeric, and lemon grass, and sauté gently for 5 minutes.

3 Drain the noodles. Add the coconut milk and broth to the pan and bring just to a boil. Reduce the heat and stir in the collard greens or cabbage, beans, mushrooms, and drained noodles. Cover with a lid and simmer for 5 minutes. Stir in the peanuts and season to taste with salt and black pepper. Serve immediately.

4 oz dried medium egg noodles
2 tablespoons vegetable oil
1 onion, chopped
1 red chile, seeded and sliced
3 garlic cloves, sliced
2 inch piece of fresh ginger root, peeled and grated
2 teaspoons ground coriander
½ teaspoon turmeric
1 lemon grass stalk, finely sliced
1¾ cups coconut milk
1¼ cups Vegetable Broth (see page 246)
2 cups finely shredded collard greens or cabbage
3 cups diagonally sliced, trimmed green beans
5 oz shiitake mushrooms, sliced
½ cup raw, unsalted peanuts
salt and black pepper

Serves 4
Prep time **15 minutes**
Cooking time **15 minutes**

EAT YOURSELF *Healthy*

Students get a rap for their unhealthy eating habits, and the combination of budget, time, and skill constraints means this is often justified. If you've been fortunate enough to be treated like a guest in a restaurant for most of your mealtimes while living at home, there has probably been little incentive to dice and slice your way to your own dinner. However, eating a balanced, healthy diet will not only sharpen your brain cells and keep you alert during the dullest lecture, it will also boost your body's immune system against coughs, colds, and viruses. Infectious bugs rampage through student households like wildfire, so if you can give yourself a head start on warding them off, so much the better.

THE HEALTHY VEGGIE

As a vegetarian, you need to do more planning and preparation than your carnivore classmates. Protein and iron are the two elements that a veggie student diet may well be lacking, so it's important to make sure you include these by eating plenty of dairy produce, eggs, and grains (for protein) and nuts, green vegetables, and dried fruit (for iron).

HIGH FIVE

Getting your five a day should be second nature to a vegetarian, because you should be substituting fish and meat for larger portions and a greater range of fresh fruit and vegetables. This is where market shopping comes into its own—supermarket produce can be surprisingly expensive for nonstaples, so it makes sense to shop around and make use of local markets and vegetable stalls.

CARB-LOADING

Carbohydrates are energy foods—and that doesn't mean sports drinks, lattes, and chocolate bars. We're talking about slow-release energy that will keep you going throughout the day instead of giving you a quick burst at breakfast time and leaving you with a sugar crash by the time you get into college. Bread, rice, and pasta are all excellent sources of cheap and nutritious carbohydrates, but you need to swap white for whole wheat types in order to get the most benefit and maximize your energy levels.

KEEP FIT

Lethargy is a common curse of the student lifestyle, and it's easy to fall into the habit of sleeping, slouching, and sitting around. If you live close to campus, you can shave pounds off your love handles and your weekly budget by ditching the bus and walking or cycling to lectures. Alternatively, swap one evening a week in the student union for an evening in the gym or at sports practice.

HOT & SPICY VEGETABLE NOODLES

2 tablespoons vegetable oil
2 garlic cloves, thinly sliced
1 mild red chile, seeded and
    finely chopped
1 bunch of scallions, sliced
2½ cups Vegetable Broth
    (see page 246)
1 tablespoon soy sauce
1 large zucchini, diced
8 baby corn, halved
3 tablespoons peeled and
    grated fresh ginger root
4 oz rice noodles
3½ cups trimmed spinach

1 Heat the oil in a large saucepan or wok, add the garlic, chile, and scallions, and sauté for 30 seconds. Stir in the broth, soy sauce, zucchini, baby corn, and ginger.

2 Bring to a boil, then reduce the heat to its lowest setting, cover with a lid, and cook gently for 10 minutes.

3 Stir in the rice noodles and cook for several minutes or until they start to soften. Add the spinach and cook for another 2–3 minutes, stirring to combine the ingredients. Serve in warm deep bowls.

Serves **2**
Prep time **10 minutes**
Cooking time **20 minutes**

STUDENT TIP

It goes without saying that you should never go the supermarket on an empty stomach. Hunger can do strange things to a budget and shopping list—before you know it, you'll have a shopping cart full of cookies and nothing to create a healthy meal.

BLACK BEAN SOUP
with Soba Noodles

1 Cook the noodles in a saucepan of boiling water for about 5 minutes, or according to the package directions, until just tender.

2 Meanwhile, heat the oil in a saucepan, add the scallions and garlic, and sauté gently for 1 minute.

3 Add the chile, ginger, black bean sauce, and broth and bring to a boil. Stir in the bok choy or collard greens, soy sauce, sugar, and peanuts, reduce the heat, and simmer gently, uncovered, for 4 minutes.

4 Drain the noodles and pile into warm serving bowls. Ladle over the soup and serve immediately.

8 oz dried soba noodles
2 tablespoons vegetable oil
1 bunch of scallions, sliced
2 garlic cloves, coarsely chopped
1 red chile, seeded and sliced
1½ inch piece of fresh ginger root, peeled and grated
½ cup black bean sauce or black bean stir-fry sauce
3 cups Vegetable Broth (see page 246)
3 cups shredded bok choy or collard greens
2 teaspoons soy sauce
1 teaspoon sugar
½ cup raw, unsalted peanuts

Serves **4**
Prep time **5 minutes**
Cooking time **10 minutes**

AFFORDABILITY
1

Rice Noodle Pancakes
WITH STIR-FRIED VEGETABLES

Ⓥ

8 oz dried ribbon rice noodles
1 green chile, seeded and sliced
1 inch piece of fresh ginger root, peeled and grated
3 tablespoons chopped fresh cilantro
2 teaspoons all-purpose flour
2 teaspoons vegetable oil, plus extra for pan-frying

Stir-fried vegetables
¼ broccoli
2 tablespoons vegetable oil
1 small onion, sliced
1 red bell pepper, cored, seeded, and sliced
1 yellow or orange bell pepper, cored, seeded, and sliced
2 cups sugar snap peas (halved lengthwise)
⅓ cup hoisin sauce
1 tablespoon lime juice
salt and black pepper

Serves 4
Prep time **15 minutes**
Cooking time **15 minutes**

1 Cook the noodles in a saucepan of lightly salted boiling water for 3 minutes, or according to the package directions, until tender. Drain well. Transfer to a bowl, then add the chile, ginger, cilantro, flour, and the 2 teaspoons oil and mix well. Set aside.

2 Thinly slice the broccoli stems and cut the florets into small pieces. Cook the brocooli stems in boiling water for 30 seconds, then add the florets and cook for another 30 seconds. Drain.

3 Heat the 2 tablespoons oil in a wok or large skillet, add the onion, and stir-fry for 2 minutes. Add the bell peppers and stir-fry for 3 minutes, until softened but still retaining texture. Stir in the cooked broccoli, sugar snap peas, hoisin sauce, and lime juice, season to taste with salt and black pepper, and set aside.

4 Heat ½ inch oil in a skillet. Place four large separate spoonfuls of the noodles (half the mixture) in the oil. Cook for about 5 minutes, until crisp and lightly browned. Drain the noodle pancakes on paper towels and keep warm while cooking the remaining noodle mixture in the same way.

5 Heat the vegetables through for 1 minute in the wok or skillet. Place two pancakes each on warm serving plates and pile the stir-fried vegetables on top.

AFFORDABILITY
1

WARM PASTA SALAD WITH
LEMON & BROCCOLI

Salads, Sides, Snacks

CHEESE & SCALLIONS
ON TOAST

BAKED SWEET POTATO

CORN & ZUCCHINI CAKES

VEGAN LUNCH BOWL SALAD

½ cup quinoa, rinsed
1 teaspoon vegan vegetable
  bouillon powder
½ red bell pepper, seeded and
  thinly sliced
½ small fennel bulb, thinly
  sliced
½ small butterhead lettuce,
  finely shredded
handful of basil leaves,
  shredded

Dressing
1 teaspoon harissa paste
3 tablespoons olive oil
2 teaspoons white or red
  wine vinegar
1 teaspoon sugar
salt

Serves **1**
Prep time **15 minutes,
plus cooling**
Cooking time **15 minutes**

1 Put the quinoa into a saucepan with the bouillon powder
and 1 cup boiling water, cover with a lid, and cook gently for
15 minutes, until the quinoa is tender and the water absorbed.
If there's still a lot of liquid in the pan, increase the heat,
remove the lid, and cook for a couple of minutes so the liquid
evaporates.

2 Transfer the quinoa to a bowl and stir in the red bell pepper
and fennel. Let cool.

3 Beat together the dressing ingredients. Stir the lettuce,
basil, and dressing into the salad to serve.

AFFORDABILITY
1

Gado Gado Salad

4 eggs
1 iceberg lettuce, coarsely chopped
2 carrots, peeled and cut into matchsticks
½ cucumber, peeled and cut into matchsticks
½ red bell pepper, cored, seeded, and cut into matchsticks

Peanut dressing
¼ cup chunky peanut butter
juice of 1 lime
1 tablespoon honey
1 tablespoon soy sauce
½ teaspoon finely chopped red chile

Serves 4
Prep time **15 minutes**
Cooking time **15 minutes**

AFFORDABILITY
1

1 Put the eggs into a saucepan of cold water and bring to a boil. Cook for 10 minutes, then plunge into cold water to cool. Shell the eggs, then cut them in half lengthwise. Combine all the remaining salad ingredients in a bowl or arrange on a plate, then add the egg halves.

2 Put all the dressing ingredients into a saucepan and heat gently, stirring, until combined. Drizzle the dressing over the salad and serve immediately or serve the dressing as a dipping sauce for the salad.

HEALTHY GREEN BEAN & BROCCOLI SALAD

3 cup mixture of broccoli florets and fine green beans
1 (15 oz) can cranberry or adzuki beans, rinsed and drained
1 celery stick, finely chopped
½ small red onion, finely sliced
1 small ripe avocado, peeled, pitted, and diced
1 tablespoon sunflower seeds

Dressing
1 tablespoon lime or lemon juice
2 tablespoons vegetable oil
1 tablespoon light soy sauce

Serves **2**
Prep time **10 minutes**
Cooking time **2-3 minutes**

1 Cook the green beans and broccoli in a saucepan of lightly salted boiling water for 2-3 minutes, until just tender. Drain and cool under cold running water, then drain again.

2 Meanwhile, combine the canned beans in a bowl with the celery, onion, and avocado.

3 Whisk together the dressing ingredients in a small bowl.

4 Add the green beans and broccoli to the salad and gently fold through the dressing. Spoon into a serving dish and sprinkle with the sunflower seeds.

MIDDLE EASTERN
BREAD SALAD

2 flour tortillas or other
  flatbreads
1 large green bell pepper, cored,
  seeded, and diced
1 Lebanese cucumber, diced
16 cherry tomatoes, halved
½ red onion, finely chopped
2 tablespoons chopped mint
2 tablespoons chopped parsley
2 tablespoons chopped fresh
  cilantro
3 tablespoons olive oil
juice of 1 lemon
salt and black pepper

Serves 4-6
Prep time **10 minutes,
plus cooling**
Cooking time **2-3 minutes**

1 Cook the tortillas or flatbreads under a preheated hot broiler for 2-3 minutes, until toasted and charred. Let cool, then tear into bite-size pieces.

2 Put the green bell pepper, cucumber, tomatoes, onion, and herbs into a bowl, add the oil, lemon juice, and salt and black pepper, and stir well. Add the bread and stir again. Serve immediately.

AFFORDABILITY
1

SWEET POTATO & *Haloumi Salad*

THIS COMBINATION OF FIRM, SALTY CHEESE, SWEET POTATO, AND A HONEYED, SPICED CITRUS DRESSING IS ABSOLUTELY DELICIOUS.

3 sweet potatoes (about 1 lb), sliced
3 tablespoons olive oil
8 oz haloumi cheese, patted dry on paper towels, or Muenster cheese
3 cups arugula

Dressing
⅓ cup olive oil
3 tablespoons honey
2 tablespoons lemon or lime juice
1½ teaspoons black onion seeds
1 red chile, seeded and finely sliced
2 teaspoons chopped lemon thyme
salt and black pepper

Serves **4**
Prep time **10 minutes**
Cooking time **15 minutes**

1 Mix together all the ingredients for the dressing in a small bowl.

2 Cook the sweet potatoes in a saucepan of lightly salted boiling water for 2 minutes. Drain well. Heat the oil in a large skillet, add the sweet potatoes, and sauté for about 10 minutes, turning once, until golden.

3 Meanwhile, thinly slice the cheese and place on a lightly oiled aluminum foil-lined broiler rack. Cook under a preheated medium broiler for about 3 minutes, until golden.

4 Pile the sweet potatoes, cheese, and arugula onto serving plates and spoon the dressing over them.

AFFORDABILITY **2**

PANZANELLA

FOR THIS SALAD, IT IS BEST TO USE SLIGHTLY STALE CIABATTA THAT WILL NOT FALL APART. ALTERNATIVELY, USE LIGHTLY TOASTED FRESH BREAD.

3 red bell peppers, cored, seeded, and quartered
6 ripe plum tomatoes, skinned
⅓ cup olive oil
3 tablespoons wine vinegar
2 garlic cloves, crushed
1 stale ciabatta roll
½ cup pitted black ripe olives
small handful of basil leaves, shredded
salt and black pepper

Serves 4
Prep time 20 minutes
Cooking time 10 minutes

1 Place the bell peppers, skin side up, on an aluminum foil-lined broiler rack and broil under a preheated medium broiler for 10 minutes or until the skins are blackened.

2 Meanwhile, quarter the tomatoes and scoop out the pulp, placing it in a strainer over a bowl to catch the juices. Set the tomato quarters aside. Press the pulp with the back of a spoon to extract as much juice as possible.

3 Beat the oil, vinegar, garlic, and salt and black pepper into the tomato juice.

4 When cool enough to handle, peel the skins from the bell peppers and discard. Coarsely slice the bell peppers and put into a bowl with the tomato quarters. Break the bread into small chunks and add to the bowl with the olives and basil.

5 Add the dressing and toss all the ingredients together before serving.

AFFORDABILITY
1

WARM EGGPLANT SALAD

2 tablespoons olive oil
2 eggplants, cut into small
   cubes
1 red onion, finely sliced
2 tablespoons capers, drained
   and coarsely chopped
4 tomatoes, chopped
¼ cup chopped parsley
1 tablespoon balsamic vinegar
salt and black pepper

Serves **4**
Prep time **10 minutes,
plus cooling**
Cooking time **10 minutes**

1 Heat the oil in a nonstick skillet, add the eggplants, and sauté for 10 minutes, until golden and softened.

2 Add the onion, capers, tomatoes, parsley, and vinegar and stir to combine. Season lightly to taste. Remove from the heat and let cool for 10 minutes before serving.

COOKING TIP

Don't throw away the last few pasta shapes in the package; save them in a food container and you'll have an eclectic mix for your next pasta dinner. Most regular pasta shapes cook in a similar amount of time, so you won't need to worry about cooking times.

AFFORDABILITY
1

Warm Pasta Salad
WITH LEMON & BROCCOLI

1 Cook the pasta in a large saucepan of lightly salted boiling water according to the package directions, adding the broccoli florets, edamame, peas, and sugar snaps for the final 3 minutes of the cooking time. Drain the pasta and vegetables, reserving a ladleful of the cooking water, then return to the pan.

2 Stir in the cream cheese, lemon zest and juice, olive oil, chile, grated cheese, tarragon, some salt and black pepper, and a splash of cooking water. Serve the salad warm or at room temperature.

12 oz dried penne or rigatoni
2 cups broccoli florets
²/₃ cup frozen edamame
  (soybeans)
²/₃ cup frozen peas
1²/₃ cups trimmed sugar
  snap peas
²/₃ cup cream cheese with
  garlic and herbs
finely grated zest and juice
  of 1 lemon
¼ cup olive oil
1 red chile, seeded and finely
  chopped
1 cup grated Parmesan-style
  cheese
2 tablespoons chopped
  tarragon
salt and black pepper

Serves **4**
Prep time **10 minutes**
Cooking time **10-12 minutes**

MUSHROOM & EGG
Fried Rice

2 tablespoons vegetable oil
3 cups chopped mushrooms
2 scallions
1 extra-large egg, beaten
2 cups cooked rice
soy sauce, to serve

Serves **2**
Prep time **5 minutes**
Cooking time **10 minutes**

1 Heat the oil in a large skillet, add the mushrooms and scallions, and stir-fry over medium heat for 4–5 minutes, until the mushrooms have softened.

2 Increase the heat and add the beaten egg to the pan. Cook for another 2 minutes, stirring frequently, until the egg is cooked.

3 Stir in the rice and heat until it is piping hot, then serve immediately with soy sauce.

AFFORDABILITY 1

STUDENT TIP

If you have a strict food budget, take only the exact amount of cash you have to spend when you go shopping. That way you won't be tempted to fill up your shopping cart with unnecessary luxuries and pile it on the credit card when you get to the checkout.

TABBOULEH
with Fruit & Nuts

IF PRUNES ARE NOT YOUR FAVORITE DRIED FRUIT, SUBSTITUTE JUST ABOUT ANY OTHER—APRICOTS, GOLDEN RAISINS OR RAISINS. FIGS, AND DATES ARE ALSO GOOD.

1 cup bulgur wheat
2/3 cup unsalted, shelled
   pistachio nuts
1 small red onion, finely
   chopped
3 garlic cloves, crushed
1/3 cup chopped flat leaf parsley
1/3 cup chopped mint
finely grated zest and juice of
   1 lemon or lime
15 pitted prunes, sliced
1/4 cup olive oil
salt and black pepper

Serves 4
Prep time 15 minutes,
plus soaking

1 Put the bulgur wheat into a bowl, cover with plenty of boiling water, and let stand for 15 minutes.

2 Meanwhile, put the pistachio nuts into a separate bowl and cover with boiling water. Let stand for 1 minute, then drain. Rub the nuts between several thicknesses of paper towels to remove most of the skins, then peel away any remaining skins with your fingers.

3 Mix the nuts with the onion, garlic, parsley, mint, lemon or lime zest and juice, and prunes in a large bowl.

4 Drain the bulgur wheat thoroughly in a strainer, pressing out as much moisture as possible with the back of a spoon. Add to the other ingredients with the oil and toss together. Season to taste with salt and black pepper and chill until ready to serve.

Mashed Sweet Potatoes & GARLIC

1 Put the sweet potatoes and smoked garlic cloves into a large saucepan, cover with cold water, and bring to a boil. Reduce the heat and simmer for 10-12 minutes, until tender, then drain well. Return the sweet potatoes and garlic to the pan and mash until smooth.

2 Set the pan over low heat, then push the mashed potatoes to one side, add the butter to the bottom of the pan, and let melt. Pour the milk onto the butter and heat for 1-2 minutes, then beat into the potatoes.

3 Stir in the parsley, season to taste with salt and black pepper, and serve.

6 sweet potatoes (about 2 lb), peeled and cut into 1 inch pieces
4-6 smoked garlic cloves, peeled but left whole
2 tablespoons salted butter
2 tablespoons milk
2 tablespoons chopped flat leaf parsley
salt and black pepper

Serves 4
Prep time 10 minutes
Cooking time 15-20 minutes

AFFORDABILITY 1

BAKED
SWEET POTATOES

AFFORDABILITY
1

4 sweet potatoes (about
  8 oz each), scrubbed
1 cup sour cream
2 scallions, trimmed and
  finely chopped
1 tablespoon chopped chives
4 tablespoons butter
salt and black pepper

Serves **4**
Prep time **5 minutes**
Cooking time **45-50 minutes**

1 Put the potatoes into a roasting pan and roast in a preheated oven, at 425°F, for 45-50 minutes, until cooked through.

2 Meanwhile, combine the sour cream, scallions, chives, and salt and black pepper in a bowl.

3 Cut the baked potatoes in half lengthwise, top with the butter and spoon the sour cream mixture on top. Serve immediately.

Crisp Parsnip CAKES

1 Cook the parsnips in a large saucepan of lightly salted boiling water for 10 minutes, until tender.

2 Meanwhile, melt the butter in a small skillet, add the garlic and thyme, and sauté gently, stirring, for 2 minutes.

3 Drain the parsnips, return to the pan, and mash thoroughly. Mash in the buttery garlic mixture and season well with salt and black pepper. Let stand until cool enough to handle. Shape the parsnip mixture into 8 patties with lightly floured hands.

4 Heat 1 tablespoon of the oil in a large skillet, add 4 of the patties, and cook for 3-4 minutes on each side, until golden brown. Transfer the patties to a baking sheet and keep warm in low oven while you repeat with the remaining oil and patties. Serve warm.

6 parsnips (about 1½ lb), peeled and chopped
4 tablespoons butter
1 garlic clove, crushed
1 tablespoon chopped thyme
flour, for dusting
2 tablespoons vegetable oil
salt and black pepper

Serves 4
Prep time **10 minutes,**
plus cooling
Cooking time **20-25 minutes**

AFFORDABILITY
1

Corn & Zucchini Cakes

1 Put the corn into a large bowl with the zucchini, cumin seeds, scallions, flour, baking powder, eggs, cilantro, chile, and some salt and black pepper and mix well.

2 Heat 1 tablespoon of the oil in a large nonstick skillet and cook spoonfuls of the batter, in batches, for 2-3 minutes on each side, until cooked through. Drain on paper towels and keep warm while cooking the remainder in the same way; the batter makes 12 cakes.

3 Serve with guacamole and lime wedges.

1 cup corn kernels, thawed if frozen
1 zucchini, coarsely grated
1 teaspoon cumin seeds
4 scallions, thinly sliced
3 tablespoons all-purpose flour
pinch of baking powder
2 eggs, beaten
2 tablespoons chopped fresh cilantro
1 red chile, seeded and coarsely chopped
vegetable oil, for frying
salt and black pepper

To serve
store-bought guacamole
lime wedges

Serves **4**
Prep time **10 minutes,**
Cooking time **15-20 minutes**

AFFORDABILITY
1

CHARGRILLED
POLENTA TRIANGLES

olive oil, for brushing
2 teaspoons salt
1 cup instant grits or polenta
2 garlic cloves, crushed
4 tablespoons butter
½ cup Parmesan-style cheese,
  grated, plus extra to serve
black pepper
chopped fresh parsley,
  to garnish

Serves 4
Prep time **5 minutes**,
plus cooling
Cooking time **20-25 minutes**

1 Lightly brush a 9 x 12 inch baking pan with oil. Bring 4 cups of water to a boil in a heavy saucepan, add the salt, and then gradually whisk in the grits or polenta in a steady stream. Cook over low heat, stirring constantly with a wooden spoon, for 5 minutes, until the grains have swelled and thickened. Remove from the heat and immediately beat in the garlic, butter, cheese, and black pepper until smooth. Pour the porridge into the pan and let cool.

2 Turn out the porridge onto a cutting board and cut into large squares, then diagonally in half into triangles. Brush the triangles with a little oil.

3 Heat a large skillet, or ridged grill pan if you have one, until hot. Add the triangles, in batches, and cook over medium-high heat for 2-3 minutes on each side, until charred and heated through. Serve immediately, sprinkled with grated cheese and chopped parsley.

AFFORDABILITY 1

Cheese & Scallions ON TOAST

1 Heat the butter in a skillet, add the scallions, and sauté for 5 minutes or until softened.

2 Reduce the heat to low and stir in the cheese, beer or broth, and mustard. Season well with black pepper, then stir slowly for 3-4 minutes or until the cheese has melted.

3 Meanwhile, toast the bread lightly on both sides and place on a broiler pan. Pour the cheese mixture over the toast and cook under a preheated hot broiler for 1 minute or until bubbling and golden. Serve with the lettuce, radishes, and tomatoes.

2 tablespoons butter
4 scallions, thinly sliced
2 cups shredded cheddar or American cheese
¼ cup beer or vegetable broth
2 teaspoons mustard
4 slices of whole wheat bread
black pepper

To serve
butterhead lettuce
cherry tomatoes
radishes

Serves **4**
Prep time **5 minutes**
Cooking time **10 minutes**

AFFORDABILITY 1

GARLIC & BEAN PÂTÉ

1 (15 oz) can great Northern
   beans, rinsed and drained
4 oz cream cheese
2 garlic cloves, chopped
3 tablespoons homemade
   (see page 249) or store-
   bought pesto
2 scallions, chopped
1 tablespoon olive oil
salt and black pepper

To serve
cucumber sticks
pita breads

Serves 4
Prep time **5 minutes**

1 Using an immersion blender, or a food processor or blender
if you have one, blend the beans, cream cheese, garlic, and
2 tablespoons of the pesto until smooth. Add the scallions,
and salt and black pepper to taste and blend for 10 seconds.

2 Spoon into a dish and chill until required. Mix the remaining
pesto with the olive oil and drizzle on top before serving
with cucumber sticks and lightly toasted pita breads cut into
thick strips.

RED CABBAGE
& BEET LENTILS

2 tablespoons vegetable oil
½ small red cabbage, thinly
   sliced
2 scallions, sliced, plus extra
   to garnish
1 beet, coarsely grated
1 teaspoon ground cumin
1½ cups cooked green lentils
salt and black pepper
plain Greek yogurt or plain
   yogurt, to serve

1 Heat the oil in a saucepan, add the red cabbage and scallions, and cook over medium heat for about 5 minutes, until just beginning to soften. Stir in the beet, then cover with a lid and cook for another 8-10 minutes, stirring occasionally, until the vegetables are tender.

2 Sprinkle with the ground cumin and stir over the heat for a minute, then add the lentils and heat until hot. Season to taste, then serve with dollops of yogurt and extra sliced scallions.

Serves **2**
Prep time **5 minutes**
Cooking time **15-20 minutes**

RED CABBAGE
COLESLAW

1 In a bowl, combine the red cabbage, beet, and apple.

2 In a separate small bowl or jar, whisk together the dressing ingredients.

3 Pour the dressing over the coleslaw and mix well to coat. Serve with warm whole wheat pita breads.

½ small red cabbage, thinly sliced
1 small beet, coarsely grated
1 small crisp, sweet apple, peeled, cored, and coarsely grated
warm whole wheat pita breads, to serve

Dressing
1 tablespoon whole-grain mustard
1 scallion, finely chopped
2 teaspoons red wine vinegar
2 tablespoons olive oil

Serves **2**
Prep time **10 minutes**

STUDENT TIP

Although it's sometimes difficult to tell which fruit and vegetables are in season, if you shop according to the season your food bill will be less. Local farmers' markets are a good place to start—the produce needs to be harvested when it's ready and sold quickly, so take advantage.

POTATO TORTILLA

⅔ cup extra virgin olive oil
6 russet or Yukon gold potatoes
  (about 1½ lb), thinly sliced
1 onion, chopped
1 each red bell pepper and green
  bell pepper, seeded and sliced
5 eggs, beaten
salt and black pepper

Serves 6
Prep time **10 minutes,
plus standing**
Cooking time **30-35 minutes**

1 Heat all but 2 tablespoons of the oil in a large nonstick
  skillet and sauté the potatoes, onion, and bell peppers, stirring
frequently, for 15 minutes, until all the vegetables are golden
and tender.

2 Mix the potato mixture with the eggs in a large bowl
  and season well with salt and black pepper. Set aside for
15 minutes. Clean the skillet.

3 Heat the remaining oil in the clean pan and pour in the
  tortilla mixture. Cook over low heat for 10 minutes, until
almost cooked through. Carefully slide the tortilla onto a large
plate, invert the skillet over the tortilla, and then flip it back into
the skillet.

4 Return the pan to the heat and cook the tortilla for another
  5 minutes, or until it is cooked on both sides. Let cool, then
serve at room temperature, cut into wedges.

CHUNKY FRENCH FRIES

8 russet potatoes (about 2 lb)
⅔ cup mild olive oil or
  peanut oil
1 teaspoon paprika
1 teaspoon celery salt
salt and black pepper

Serves 4
Prep time **10 minutes**
Cooking time **50 minutes**

1 Cut the potatoes into ½ inch slices, then cut each slice into
  chunky sticks.

2 Brush a large roasting pan with a little of the oil and heat
  it in a preheated oven, at 425°F, for 5 minutes.

3 Spread out the potatoes in the pan, drizzle with the
  remaining oil, and sprinkle with the paprika and celery
salt. Mix until well coated and bake for 45 minutes, turning the
potaotes occasionally, until they are golden. Serve sprinkled
with salt and black pepper.

What's for Dessert?

CHOCOLATE ICE BOX CAKE

BANANA & CARAMEL LAYERS

STRAWBERRY CRUSH

Instant Mixed
BERRY SORBET

2½ cups frozen mixed berries,
  such as hulled strawberries,
  raspberries, and blueberries
1¼ cups raspberry yogurt
⅓ cup confectioners' sugar

....

Serves 4
Prep time 5 minutes

....

1 Using an immersion blender, or a food processor or
blender if you have one, blend the berries, yogurt, and
sugar until blended.

2 Scrape the mixture from the sides of the bowl and
blend again.

3 Spoon into chilled glasses or bowls and serve immediately.

Frozen Fruit PIE

1 Grease an 8 x 10 inch shallow ovenproof dish, then pour in the frozen fruit with ¼ cup of the sugar.

2 Beat together the remaining sugar, butter or margarine, eggs, flour, and baking powder in a bowl until smooth. Spoon the mixture over the fruit and smooth down evenly.

3 Bake in a preheated oven, at 400°F, for 20-25 minutes, until risen and golden, then serve with vanilla ice cream.

1 stick butter or margarine, softened, plus extra for greasing
1 (1 lb) package mixed frozen fruit
1 cup sugar
2 eggs
1 cup all-purpose flour
1 teaspoon baking powder
vanilla ice cream, to serve

Serves 4-6
Prep time **10 minutes**
Cooking time **20-25 minutes**

AFFORDABILITY
1

MIXED FRUITS WITH HONEYED OAT TOPPING

1 Put the apricots and strawberries into a bowl. Add the Greek yogurt and honey and sprinkle the oats and almonds over the top.

4 apricots, halved and pitted
4 strawberries, hulled and
 halved
2 teaspoons honey
1 tablespoon Greek yogurt
1 tablespoon medium rolled oats
1 tablespoon toasted almonds

Serves 1
Prep time **5 minutes**

COOKING TIP

Use freezer stickers to record the food and the date. You'll be pleased you made the effort in a few months' time when you're hungry but have no idea what the bag of frozen mush is at the back of the freezer, or how long it's been there.

AFFORDABILITY
1

Strawberry CRUSH

12 oz strawberries, hulled
1 tablespoon confectioners' sugar
1¼ cups low-fat fromage blanc or Greek yogurt
4 store-bought meringue nests
4 lavender sprigs, to decorate (optional)

Serves **4**
Prep time **5 minutes**

1 Using a fork, or a food processor or blender if you have one, mash the strawberries with the confectioners' sugar.

2 Put the fromage blanc in a bowl, crumble in the meringues, and mix together lightly.

3 Add the strawberry mixture and fold together with a spoon until marbled. Spoon into glasses and serve decorated with lavender sprigs, if using.

AFFORDABILITY 1

NUTTY
PASSION FRUIT
YOGURTS

1 Halve the passion fruits and scoop the pulp into a large bowl. Add the yogurt and mix together gently.

2 Put 1 tablespoonful of honey in the bottom of each of two narrow glasses and sprinkle a few hazelnuts over it. Spoon half the yogurt over the nuts and arrange half the clementine pieces on top.

3 Repeat the layering, finishing with a few hazelnuts on the top of the dish. Chill until ready to serve.

2 passion fruits
1 cup plain yogurt
2 tablespoons honey
¼ cup coarsely chopped hazelnuts
4 clementines, peeled and chopped into small pieces

Serves **2**
Prep time **5 minutes**

AFFORDABILITY
2

BANANA & CARAMEL
LAYERS

6 graham crackers or
  shortbread cookies, crushed
2 large bananas
4 tablespoons butter
¼ cup packed dark brown sugar
⅔ cup heavy cream
1 cup crème fraîche or plain
  Greek yogurt
grated semisweet chocolate,
  to decorate

Serves 4
Prep time **10 minutes**
Cooking time **5 minutes**

1 Divide the cookie crumbs among four tall serving glasses and use to line each bottom. Mash one of the bananas and divide among the glasses, spooning on top of the cookie crumbs.

2 Melt the butter in a small saucepan, add the sugar, and heat over medium heat, stirring well, until the sugar has dissolved. Add the cream and cook gently for 1-2 minutes, until the mixture is thick. Remove from the heat and let cool for 1 minute, then spoon on top of the mashed banana.

3 Slice the second banana and arrange on top of the caramel, then spoon over the crème fraîche or yogurt. Decorate with grated chocolate before serving.

AFFORDABILITY 1

MANGO & MINT *Carpaccio* Ⓥ

⅓ cup sugar
finely grated zest and juice
  of 1 large lime
2 tablespoons finely chopped
  mint leaves, plus extra leaves
  to decorate
4 firm, ripe mangoes

Serves 4
Prep time **10 minutes**,
plus cooling
Cooking time **5 minutes**

1 Put the sugar into a small saucepan with the lime zest and juice, mint, and ⅓–½ cup of water. Bring to a boil and remove from the heat. Stir until the sugar is dissolved. Let cool.

2 Meanwhile, cut the mangoes in half, running a sharp knife around the pits to detach. Peel and slice as thinly as possible.

3 Arrange the mango slices on serving plates and drizzle with the sugar syrup. Serve decorated with mint leaves.

AFFORDABILITY 2

Ⓥ PINEAPPLE WITH LIME & CHILI SYRUP

½ cup sugar
3 red chiles, seeded and finely diced
grated zest and juice of 1 lime
1 small pineapple, halved or quartered, cored, and cut into wafer-thin slices

....

Serves **4**
Prep time **10 minutes**, plus cooling
Cooking time **10 minutes**

....

1 Put the sugar and ½ cup of water into a saucepan and heat slowly until the sugar has dissolved, then add the chiles, bring to a boil, and boil rapidly until the liquid becomes syrupy. Let cool.

2 Stir the lime zest and juice into the cooled syrup. Lay the pineapple slices on a plate and drizzle the syrup over the fruit. Serve chilled.

CREAMY
CHOCOLATE

10 oz semisweet chocolate,
 broken up
2 cups fromage blanc or
 Greek yogurt
1 teaspoon vanilla extract

Serves **6**
Prep time **5 minutes**

1 Melt the chocolate in a heatproof bowl set over a saucepan
 of simmering water (do not let the bowl touch the water),
then remove from the heat. Add the fromage blanc or yogurt
and the vanilla extract and quickly stir together.

2 Divide the creamy chocolate among little mugs, dishes,
 or glasses and serve immediately.

AFFORDABILITY
1

QUICK Tiramisu

1   Mix the coffee with 2 tablespoons of the sugar and the liqueur, brandy, or juice in medium bowl. Toss the ladyfingers in the mixture and turn into a serving dish, spooning over any excess liquid.

2   Beat together the pudding or custard, mascarpone, and vanilla extract and spoon one-third over the cookies. Sprinkle with the remaining sugar, then half the remaining pudding or custard. Sprinkle with the chopped chocolate, then spread with the remaining pudding or custard.

3   Chill for about 1 hour until set and serve lightly dusted with cocoa powder.

AFFORDABILITY
3

⅓ cup strong espresso coffee

⅓ cup packed dark brown sugar

¼ cup coffee liqueur or 3 tablespoons brandy or ¼ cup white grape juice or apple juice

6 ladyfinger cookies, broken into large pieces

1⅓ cups freshly prepared vanilla pudding or custard

1 cup mascarpone cheese

1 teaspoon vanilla extract

2 oz semisweet chocolate, finely chopped

unsweetened cocoa powder, for dusting

Serves 4-6
Prep time **15 minutes, plus chilling**

Almost-Instant
PEACH TRIFLE

1 Line the bottom of a glass serving dish with the cake slices. Drizzle with ½ cup of the reserved juice, then sprinkle with the sliced peaches.

2 Beat the mascarpone with the pudding or custard and confectioners' sugar, then spoon it over the fruit.

3 Spoon the whipped cream over the top, then decorate with the grated chocolate.

6 oz raspberry jellyroll, sliced, or pound cake, sliced and spread with raspberry preserves

1 (15 oz) can sliced peaches in juice, drained, juice reserved

¾ cup mascarpone cheese

1 cup freshly prepared vanilla pudding or custard

2 tablespoons confectioners' sugar

⅔ cup heavy cream, whipped

3 tablespoons grated semisweet chocolate, to decorate

Serves **4**
Prep time **10 minutes**

AFFORDABILITY
1

Chocolate
ICE BOX CAKE

As delicious as it is filling, this isn't the kind of cake you'd serve in chunky slices. Rich and intensely chocolaty, it's a treat cut into small pieces and served with coffee.

1 Line a dampened 8½ x 4½ x 2½ inch loaf pan with plastic wrap. Melt the semisweet chocolate with the butter in a heatproof bowl set over a saucepan of simmering water (do not let the bowl touch the water), stirring frequently, then let stand until cool but not beginning to harden.

2 Stir the cookies, nuts, and caramel bar into the melted mixture until combined. Turn into the pan and pack down in an even layer. Chill for several hours or overnight until set.

3 To serve, lift away the pan and let the cake soften a little at room temperature so it's easier to slice. Peel away the plastic wrap and serve in small pieces.

10 oz semisweet chocolate, broken up

6 tablespoons unsalted butter

8 shortbread cookies, broken into small pieces

1 cup whole mixed nuts, such as almonds, hazelnuts, and Brazil nuts

1 (5 oz) milk chocolate caramel bar, broken into sections

Makes **10 pieces**
Prep time **10 minutes,
plus chilling**

RICH CHOCOLATE MOUSSE

1 Melt the chocolate with the cream in a heatproof bowl set over a saucepan of simmering water (do not let the bowl touch the water), stirring frequently, until smooth. Let cool for 5 minutes, then beat in the egg yolks one at a time.

2 Whisk the egg whites in a separate clean bowl until stiff, then lightly fold into the chocolate mixture until combined. Spoon the mousse into small dishes, glasses, or cups and chill for 2 hours. Dust with cocoa powder before serving.

6 oz semisweet chocolate, broken into pieces
½ cup heavy cream
3 eggs, separated
unsweetened cocoa powder, for dusting

Serves 4
Prep time 10 minutes, plus chilling

AFFORDABILITY
1

Strawberry Cheesecake MUG CAKE

⬤ ⬤

⅓ cup cream cheese
2 teaspoons sugar
1 egg yolk
2 tablespoons light cream
   or milk
2 teaspoons strawberry
   preserves or jam
handful of strawberries, hulled
   and halved, to serve
1 gingersnap cookie, crushed

Serves 1
Prep time **5 minutes, plus cooling**
Cooking time **2 minutes**

1 Choose a small microwave-proof mug with a capacity of at least ¾ cup. You can test whether a mug is suitable for the microwave by filling it with cold water and microwaving on full power for 1 minute. If the water heats up but the mug doesn't get hot, it's fine to use.

2 Put the cream cheese and sugar into the mug and beat with a small whisk or spoon until the cream cheese softens. Beat in the egg yolk and cream or milk.

3 Dot the preserves or jam over the surface. Cut through the preserves with a knife several times so it is marbled into the cream cheese without being completely blended. Microwave on medium power for 1 minute. The edges of the cheesecake should be set while the center should be loose. If the edges haven't set, return the mug to the microwave for another 15-30 seconds. Let cool.

4 Pile the strawberries on top of the cheesecake and sprinkle with the cookie crumbs to serve.

AFFORDABILITY 1

MICROWAVE CAKES
in Syrup

1 stick butter, softened, plus
    extra for greasing
½ cup packed light brown sugar
¾ cup all-purpose flour
¾ teaspoon baking powder
1 teaspoon allspice
1 egg, beaten
¼ cup light corn syrup
whipped cream, to serve

Serves **4**
Prep time **10 minutes**
Cooking time **5-7 minutes**

1 Lightly grease four ⅔ cup ramekins and line the bottoms with nonstick parchment paper. Beat together the butter and sugar in a bowl until pale and fluffy, then sift in the flour, baking powder, and spice and add the egg. Beat together until well mixed.

2 Divide the batter among the ramekins. Cover each with a disk of parchment paper and cook together in a microwave on high for 2-2½ minutes, then let the sponges rest for 3-4 minutes to finish cooking.

3 Turn the cakes out onto a serving plates and drizzle each with 1 tablespoon of the corn syrup while still warm. Serve with whipped cream.

Baked Toffee Apples

1 Toss the apples in a shallow ovenproof dish with the 1 tablespoon flour and the brown sugar.

2 Mix the remaining flour with the baking powder, granulated sugar, and spice in a bowl. Add the egg, yogurt, and butter and stir lightly until only just combined.

3 Spoon the mixture over the apples and bake in a preheated oven, at 425°F, for 15-20 minutes, until just firm and golden. Serve warm.

3 crisp, sweet apples, cored and thickly sliced
3/4 cup all-purpose flour, plus 1 tablespoon extra
3/4 teaspoon baking powder
1/2 cup packed light brown sugar
1/4 cup granulated sugar
1/2 teaspoon ground allspice
1 egg
1 1/4 cups plain yogurt
4 tablespoons unsalted butter, melted

Serves **4**
Prep time **10 minutes**
Cooking time **15-20 minutes**

STUDENT TIP

Ditch the takeouts and cook your own curry; you'll need a few basic spices and vegetarian curry pastes among your staples, but after the initial investment you'll save a fortune every time you cook your own instead of dialing for a takeout.

AFFORDABILITY 2

SYRUPY PEARS &
Choc Crumb Topping

1 Place half of the sugar in a skillet with ²/₃ cups water and the raisins and cinnamon. Bring just to a boil, add the pears, and simmer gently, uncovered, for about 5 minutes, until the pears are slightly softened.

2 Meanwhile, melt the butter in a separate skillet or saucepan, add the oats, and sauté gently for 2 minutes. Stir in the remaining sugar and cook over gentle heat until golden.

3 Spoon the pears onto warm serving plates. Stir the hazelnuts and chocolate into the oats mixture. Once the chocolate starts to melt, spoon the mixture over the pears. Serve topped with whipped cream or Greek yogurt, if desired.

¼ cup packed light brown sugar
2 tablespoons raisins
½ teaspoon ground cinnamon
4 ripe Bosc pears, peeled, halved, and cored
3 tablespoons unsalted butter
½ cup rolled oats
¼ cup coarsely chopped hazelnuts
2 oz semisweet or milk chocolate, chopped
lightly whipped cream or Greek yogurt, to serve (optional)

Serves 4
Prep time 5 minutes
Cooking time 10 minutes

AFFORDABILITY 2

WARM SPICED PLUMS

1 Put the plums, sugar, spices, and 3 tablespoons of water into a large, heavy saucepan and bring to a boil, stirring occasionally.

2 Reduce the heat to low, cover with a lid, and simmer gently for 15-20 minutes, stirring occasionally, until the plums are tender. Transfer to a large serving dish and let cool for 5 minutes before serving with scoops of ice cream.

12 ripe plums (about 1½ lb), halved and pitted
½ cup sugar
½ teaspoon ground cinnamon
½ teaspoon ground ginger
vanilla ice cream, to serve

Serves 4
Prep time **5 minutes**
Cooking time **20-25 minutes**

AFFORDABILITY
1

Fruity
BAKED APPLES

4 large crisp, sweet apples
1 cup dried fruit, such as
  cranberries, golden raisins,
  and apricots
4 teaspoons raw sugar

1 Core the apples and score a line around the middle of the
  fruit and arrange them in an ovenproof dish. Stuff the cored
  center of the apples with the dried fruit.

2 Sprinkle with the sugar and bake in a preheated oven, at
  400°F, for 25 minutes or until the apples are tender.

Serves **4**
Prep time **5 minutes**
Cooking time **25 minutes**

AFFORDABILITY **1**

Rhubarb & Raspberry
CRISP

1 lb fresh or frozen rhubarb,
  thawed if frozen, sliced
1 cup fresh or frozen
  raspberries
¼ cup packed light brown sugar
3 tablespoons orange juice
raspberry ripple ice cream, to
  serve

Crumb topping
1⅔ cups all-purpose flour
pinch of salt
1¼ sticks cold unsalted butter,
  diced, plus extra for greasing
¼ cup packed light brown sugar

Serves **4**
Prep time **10 minutes**
Cooking time **25 minutes**

1 Make the crumb topping. Put the flour and salt into a bowl, add the butter, and rub in with the fingertips until the mixture resembles bread crumbs. Stir in the sugar.

2 Mix the fruits, sugar, and orange juice together in a separate bowl, then transfer to a greased ovenproof dish. Sprinkle over the topping and bake in a preheated oven, at 400°F, for about 25 minutes or until golden brown and bubbling. Serve the crisp hot with raspberry ripple ice cream.

AFFORDABILITY
2

RAISIN CAKES
WITH SYRUP

1 Grease an 8 x 10 inch shallow ovenproof dish, then pour in the corn syrup.

2 Beat the remaining ingredients together until pale and creamy and spoon the batter over the syrup in the dish. Bake in a preheated oven, at 400°F, for 20-25 minutes or until risen and golden. Serve with whipped cream or ice cream, if desired.

1 stick butter, softened, plus extra for greasing
⅓ cup light corn syrup
1 cup all-purpose flour
1 teaspoon baking powder
⅔ cup sugar
2 extra-large eggs
1 teaspoon vanilla extract (optional)
½ cup raisins
whipped cream or ice cream, to serve (optional)

Serves **6**
Prep time **5 minutes**
Cooking time **20-25 minutes**

STUDENT TIP

Now that most big supermarkets seem to be open 24/7, it's not as easy to pick up a closing-time bargain as it used to be. But if you hang around near the end of the day, you can still grab some good deals— just make sure you buy food that you are actually going to eat.

Choc Cinnamon
FRENCH TOAST

2 eggs, lightly beaten
2 thick slices of seeded whole
   wheat bread, cut in half
1 tablespoon butter
2 tablespoons sugar
2 teaspoons unsweetened
   cocoa powder
½ teaspoon ground cinnamon

Serves **2**
Prep time **5 minutes**
Cooking time **4 minutes**

1 Put the eggs into a shallow dish. Press the bread into the egg mixture, turning to coat well.

2 Melt the butter in a heavy skillet and add the egg-coated bread. Cook for 3 minutes, turning as needed.

3 Mix the sugar, cocoa powder, and cinnamon on a plate and place the hot egg-coated toast on top, turning to coat. Serve immediately.

AFFORDABILITY
1

SPICY CARROT &
PINEAPPLE JUICE

Bar, Drinks, Basics

MIXED BERRY SMOOTHIE

TEQUILA SUNRISE ICE POPS

PIMM'S COCKTAIL

1 Fill a tall glass with ice cubes. Pour all the remaining ingredients, one by one in order, over the ice.

2 Decorate with cucumber strips, blueberries, and orange wheels and serve.

(V)

ice cubes
1 measure Pimm's No 1
1 measure gin
2 measures lemon-flavor soda
2 measures ginger ale
cucumber strips, blueberries
  and orange wheels, to
  decorate

Serves **1**
Prep time **3 minutes**

SANGRIA (V)

ice cubes
6 measures Spanish brandy
8 measures fresh orange juice
2 cups red wine
1 liter club soda or lemon-flavor
  soda
orange slices and cinnamon
  sticks, to decorate

Serves **6**
Prep time **5 minutes**

1 Put a small number of ice cubes in a large pitcher. Pour the brandy, orange juice, and wine over the ice and stir well.

2 Add more ice, top up with club soda or lemon-flavor soda, and decorate with orange slices and cinnamon sticks. Serve in ice-filled wine glasses.

MOJITO

THIS IS A COOLING, EFFERVESCENT COCKTAIL BORN—THANKS TO PROHIBITION—AMID CUBA'S THRIVING INTERNATIONAL BAR CULTURE. IT PROBABLY DERIVED FROM THE MINT JULEP.

12 mint leaves, plus an extra
  sprig to decorate
½ measure sugar syrup
  (see page 243)
4 lime wedges
crushed ice
2 measures white rum
club soda, to top up

1 Put the mint, sugar syrup, and lime wedges into a tall glass and muddle together (see below).

2 Fill the glass with crushed ice, pour the rum over the ice, and stir. Top up with club soda. Decorate with a mint sprig and serve with straws.

Serves 1
Prep time 2 minutes

TECHNIQUE: *Muddling*

This is used to bring out the flavors of fruit and herbs using a muddler (the rounded end of a wooden spoon handle works, too). A famous example is the Mojito, where mint, sugar syrup ,and lime wedges are muddled in the bottom of a tall glass before the remaining ingredients are added.

Remove the mint leaves from their stems and put them into the bottom of a tall glass.

Add the sugar syrup and lime wedges. Hold the glass firmly with one hand and use the muddler to press down on the mint and lime wedges. Twist the muddler and press firmly to release the flavor of the mint and to break it down with the juice from the lime wedges. Continue this process for about 30 seconds, then top up the glass with crushed ice. Add the remaining ingredients to the glass, as specified in the recipe.

White RUSSIAN

THIS MODERN TAKE ON THE BLACK RUSSIAN USES TIA MARIA AND CREAM TO GIVE THE DRINK ITS DISTINCTIVE COLOR AND TEXTURE.

6 ice cubes, cracked
1 measure vodka
1 measure Tia Maria
1 measure whole milk or
  heavy cream

1 Put half the cracked ice into a cocktail shaker and put the remaining cracked ice into a tall glass.

2 Add all the remaining ingredients to the shaker and shake until a frost forms on the outside of the shaker. Strain over the ice in the glass. Serve with a straw.

Serves 1
Prep time **2 minutes**

Cosmopolitan

MANY PEOPLE HAVE CLAIMED TO BEING THE INVENTOR OF THE COSMOPOLITAN; HOWEVER, IT IS A RELATIVELY RECENT COCKTAIL THAT HAS BECOME SOMETHING OF A CLASSIC ALREADY.

1 Put the cracked ice into a cocktail shaker. Add all the remaining ingredients and shake until a frost forms on the outside of the shaker.

2 Strain into a chilled Martini (cocktail) glass. Decorate with an orange zest twist and serve.

6 ice cubes, cracked
1 measure vodka
½ measure Cointreau
1 measure cranberry juice
freshly squeezed juice of ½ lime
orange zest twist, to decorate

Serves 1
Prep time **2 minutes**

TECHNIQUE: *Shaking*

Shaking is used to mix ingredients quickly and thoroughly and to chill the drink before serving.

Fill the cocktail shaker or the Boston glass (if using a Boston shaker) halfway with ice cubes (or the amount specified in the recipe) or add cracked or crushed ice. If the recipe calls for a chilled glass, add a few ice cubes and some water to the glass and swirl them around before discarding. Add the remaining ingredients to the shaker. Put on the strainer and cap or, if using a Boston shaker, place the shaking cup over the glass. Shake until condensation forms on the outside of the shaker. Use both hands to hold each end of the shaker and to prevent it from slipping from your grip. The cocktail is then ready to be strained into the glass for serving by removing the cap but keeping the strainer in place.

TEQUILA SUNRISE ICE POPS

WHEN YOU POUR THE CASSIS MIXTURE INTO THE MOLDS, YOU WANT IT TO FLOAT ON TOP AND SLIGHTLY BLEND IN WITH THE TEQUILA BASE, SO THE TEQUILA NEEDS TO BE ALMOST FROZEN BUT STILL A LITTLE SLUSHY.

½ cup lemon juice
⅔ cup superfine sugar
¼ cup tequila
½ cup club soda
1 tablespoon crème de cassis

(V)

Makes **4**
Prep time **10 minutes**,
plus freezing
Cooking time **10 minutes**

1 Put the lemon juice and sugar into a saucepan with ½ cup of water and slowly bring to a boil, letting the sugar dissolve. Let simmer for 5 minutes, then remove from the heat.

2 Pour in the tequila and club soda and mix well to combine. Measure out ⅓ cup of the mixture and set aside. Divide the remaining mixture among four ice pop molds. Place the molds in the freezer for 4 hours.

3 Combine the reserved mixture with the cassis. After the 4 hours are up, remove the ice pops from the freezer and pour the cassis mixture into the molds. Insert the ice pop sticks and freeze for another 4-6 hours, until completely solid.

Drinking RESPONSIBLY

With some exceptions, the legal age for drinking alcohol in most U.S. states is 21 years old, so most students won't be legally old enough to drink until their senior year as an undergraduate. Once you are old enough to indulge, try to avoid the temptation to overdo a night out. It may take some trial and error before you learn your limits. Meanwihle, here are a few tips to ease you into the morning after.

LINE YOUR STOMACH

The fact is that if you drink too much alcohol, you'll pay for it the next day. But if you eat before you start knocking back the beers, you have a better chance of being able to remain standing by the end of the evening. Pasta is the obvious choice because it's full of slow-burning carbs that should help to soak up some of the alcohol. Other helpful hangover-busting ingredients include bread, eggs, and milk.

DROWN YOUR SORROWS

If you alternate each alcoholic drink with a large glass of water, you'll not only keep your body hydrated (alcohol is dehydrating, which is partly to blame for the pounding headache the next morning), but you'll also slow down your alcohol consumption.

WALK IT OFF

If you spend your taxi or bus money in the bar and end up having to walk home, you could actually be doing your hangover a favor. A brisk walk before you crash out in bed can help to start removing the alcohol from your system and you'll begin to sober up on the way home.

FORCE DOWN A BIG BREAKFAST

There's a good reason why people dig into bacon and eggs when they're feeling the after effects of a night on the town. Eggs contain an amino acid that can help to rid your body of toxins, while the fat and salt will replace vital minerals and should help to make you feel slightly more human.

BACK TO BED

Students are notoriously good at sleeping, so take the opportunity to live up to your reputation and wipe out the day by staying in bed. Keep a bottle of water on hand so you can rehydrate between power naps, and when the thought of food no longer makes you feel nauseous, try a plain piece of toast or a plain cookie to reacquaint your stomach with food.

SPICY CARROT & PINEAPPLE JUICE

4 carrots
½ small chile, seeded
¼ pineapple, skinned and cored
ice cubes
juice of ½ lime
1 tablespoon chopped cilantro
  leaves

Serves 1
Prep time 10 minutes

1 Juice the carrots with the chile and pineapple. If you are using a blender, chop the vegetables and fruit into small pieces and pass through a strainer after blending.

2 Pour the juice into a glass over ice. Squeeze the lime juice over the top, stir in the chopped cilantro, and serve immediately.

MIXED BERRY SMOOTHIE

1 small ripe banana, coarsely
  chopped
1½ cups fresh mixed berries,
  such as hulled strawberries,
  raspberries, and blueberries
1 cup vanilla yogurt
about ⅔ cup milk

Serves 2
Prep time 5 minutes

1 Using an immersion blender, or a food processor or blender if you have one, blend the banana, berries, yogurt, and milk and until thick and smooth, adding a little more milk if you prefer a thinner consistency.

2 Pour the smoothie into glasses and serve immediately.

CRANBERRY & APPLE SMOOTHIE

2 small apples
²/₃ cup frozen cranberries
½ cup plain yogurt
1 tablespoon honey
ice cubes (optional)

1 Juice the apples. If you are using a blender, chop into small pieces and pass through a strainer after blending. Briefly blend the juice with the cranberries, yogurt, and honey in a food processor or blender or using an immersion blender.

2 Pour the smoothie into a glass over ice, if using, and serve immediately.

Serves **1**
Prep time **5 minutes**

Classic LEMONADE

½ cup sugar syrup (see below)
1 cup fresh lemon juice
lemon slices, to decorate

1 Mix the ingredients with 4 cups of cold water in a bowl and stir well. Transfer to an airtight container and chill thoroughly in the refrigerator. Stir regularly and drink within 3 days of preparing.

2 Serve in tall glasses, decorated with lemon slices.

Serves **10**
Prep time **10 minutes,**
plus chilling

TECHNIQUE:
Sugar Syrup

This is used as a sweetener in many cocktails and drinks. It blends into a cold drink more quickly than sugar and adds body. You can buy it in bottles, but it's easy to make your own. Simply bring equal quantities of granulated sugar and water to a boil in a small saucepan, stirring constantly, then boil for 1–2 minutes without stirring. Sugar syrup can be kept in a sterilized jar in the refrigerator for up to 2 months.

ORANGE & RASPBERRY JUICE

V

1 Peel the oranges and divide the flesh into segments. Juice the orange segments with the raspberries. If you are using a blender, pass the juice through a strainer after blending. Add 1 cup of water.

2 Pour the juice into tall glasses over ice, if using, and serve immediately.

2 large oranges
1½ cups raspberries
ice cubes (optional)

Serves **2**
Prep time **5 minutes**

APPLE, APRICOT & PEACH JUICE

1 Juice the apples with the apricots and peach. If you are using a blender, chop the fruit into pieces and pass through a strainer after blending.

2 Blend the juice with a few ice cubes in a food processor or blender, or using an immersion blender, for 10 seconds. Pour the juice into a glass, decorate with peach slices, if desired, and serve immediately.

2 apples
3 apricots, halved and pitted
1 peach, halved and pitted, plus extra to serve (optional)
ice cubes

Serves **1**
Prep time **10 minutes**

FRUITY *Milk Shake*

1 ripe peach, halved, pitted, and
   chopped
1 cup hulled strawberries
1 cup raspberries
1 cup soy milk
ice cubes, to serve

Serves **2**
Prep time **2 minutes**

1 Using an immersion blender, or a food processor or blender
   if you have one, blend the peach with the strawberries and
raspberries to a smooth puree, scraping the mixture down from
the sides of the bowl, if necessary.

2 Add the soy milk and blend the ingredients again until the
   mixture is smooth and frothy. Pour the milk shake over the
ice cubes in tall glasses.

V

BANANA LASSI

3 ripe bananas, coarsely
   chopped
2 cups plain yogurt
1–2 tablespoons sugar
¼ teaspoon ground cardamom
   seeds, plus extra for
   decorating (optional)

Serves **4**
Preparation time **10 minutes**

1 Put all the ingredients in a food processor or blender and
   blend until smooth.

2 Pour into tall glasses and serve chilled, decorated with
   extra cardamom seeds, if desired. This makes an ideal
breakfast drink.

VEGETABLE BROTH

YOU CAN USE ALMOST ANY MIXTURE OF VEGETABLES, BUT THEY MUST BE REALLY FRESH. MAKE SURE YOU INCLUDE SOME ONION, BUT AVOID VEGETABLES WITH STRONG FLAVORS, SUCH AS CABBAGE, AND STARCHY ONES, SUCH AS POTATOES, WHICH WILL MAKE THE BROTH CLOUDY. FOR A DARK BROTH, LEAVE THE SKINS ON THE ONIONS AND USE PLENTY OF MUSHROOMS.

1 Heat the oil in a large, heavy saucepan and gently sauté all the vegetables for 5 minutes. Add 6½ cups cold water, the bouquet garni, and peppercorns and bring slowly to a boil.

2 Reduce the heat and simmer the broth gently for 40 minutes, skimming the surface from time to time, if necessary.

3 Strain the broth through a large strainer, preferably a conical one, and let cool. Don't squeeze the juice out of the vegetables or the broth will be cloudy.

4 Let the broth cool completely, then chill.

1 tablespoon
   vegetable oil
2 onions, coarsely
   chopped
2 carrots, coarsely
   chopped
2 celery sticks, coarsely
   chopped
1 lb mixture other vegetables,
   such as parsnips, fennel,
   leeks, zucchini, mushrooms,
   and tomatoes
1 bouquet garni
1 teaspoon black peppercorns

Makes **about 4 cups**
Prep time **10 minutes**
Cooking time **50 minutes**

Veggie Gravy

1 Heat the oil in a skillet, add the onions and sugar, and sauté for about 5 minutes, until deep golden.

2 Add the beer or juice and broth, then season to taste with salt and black pepper. Cook for 5 minutes, stirring frequently.

1 tablespoon vegetable oil
2 onions, sliced
2 teaspoons sugar
1 cup stout or apple or white
   grape juice
2/3 cup Vegetable Broth
   (see above)
salt and black pepper

Serves **4**
Prep time **5 minutes**
Cooking time **10 minutes**

TOMATO SAUCE

3 tablespoons vegetable oil
2 red onions, finely sliced
2 garlic cloves, crushed and
   chopped
2 (14½ oz) cans diced tomatoes
1 teaspoon red wine vinegar
pinch of sugar
salt and black pepper

1 Heat the oil in a large saucepan, add the onions and garlic, and sauté for 3 minutes.

2 Add the tomatoes, vinegar, sugar, and a dash of salt and black pepper and simmer until reduced to a rich tomato sauce.

Serves 4
Prep time **5 minutes**
Cooking time **15 minutes**

White Sauce

1 Put the milk in a saucepan with the onion, bay leaf, peppercorns, and parsley sprigs and bring almost to the boil. Remove the pan from the heat and let steep for 20 minutes. Strain the milk through a strainer into a bowl.

2 Melt the butter in a heavy saucepan until bubbling. Add the flour and stir quickly to combine. Cook the mixture gently, stirring constantly with a wooden spoon, for 1–2 minutes to make a smooth, pale roux (paste).

3 Remove the pan from the heat and gradually whisk in the warm milk, stirring constantly until the sauce is completely smooth. Return the pan to medium heat and cook, stirring, until the sauce comes to a boil.

4 Reduce the heat to low and continue to cook the sauce for about 5 minutes, stirring frequently until it is smooth and glossy and thinly coats the back of the spoon. Season to taste with salt, black pepper, and plenty of grated nutmeg.

1¼ cups whole milk
½ small onion
1 bay leaf
½ teaspoon peppercorns
3-4 parsley sprigs
1 tablespoon butter
2 tablespoons all-purpose flour
pinch of grated nutmeg
salt and black pepper

Serves 4
Prep time **10 minutes,
plus steeping**
Cooking time **10 minutes**

RICH CHEESE SAUCE

THIS SMOOTH AND CREAMY CHEESE SAUCE IS BOTH
SIMPLE AND DELICIOUS, AND IDEAL FOR USING UP
LEFTOVER CHEESE. YOU CAN VARY THE RECIPE WITH
PIECES OF SWISS OR BLUE CHEESE, OR COMBINE
SEVERAL DIFFERENT CHEESES.

1 Follow steps 1, 2, and 3 of White Sauce (see page 247), omitting the black peppercorns and parsley.

2 Using a mortar and pestle, lightly crush the green peppercorns until they are broken into small pieces. Alternatively, put them in a plastic food bag and crush with the back of a spoon. Add them to the sauce with the cheeses and a little nutmeg. Cook over gentle heat, stirring frequently, for about 5 minutes, until smooth and glossy. Adjust the seasoning and serve hot.

1¼ cups whole milk
½ small onion
1 bay leaf
1 tablespoon butter
2 tablespoons all-purpose flour
1 teaspoon green peppercorns, rinsed and drained
¾ cup shredded sharp cheddar cheese
¼ cup grated Parmesan-style cheese
pinch of grated nutmeg
salt

Serves **4**
Prep time **10 minutes,**
plus infusing
Cooking time **10 minutes**

PARSLEY SAUCE

¼ cup curly parsley (tough stems removed)
1 cup Vegetable Broth (see page 246)
2 tablespoons butter
3 tablespoons all-purpose flour
1 cup whole milk
3 tablespoons light cream
salt and black pepper

Serves **4**
Prep time **10 minutes**
Cooking time **10 minutes**

1 Blend the parsley with half the broth in a food processor or blender, or using an immersion blender, until the parsley is finely chopped.

2 Melt the butter in a heavy saucepan until bubbling. Add the flour and stir quickly to combine. Cook the mixture gently, stirring constantly with a wooden spoon, for 2 minutes.

3 Remove the pan from the heat and gradually whisk in the parsley-flavored broth, then the remaining broth, until smooth. Whisk in the milk. Return to the heat and bring to a boil, stirring. Reduce the heat and continue to cook the sauce for about 5 minutes, stirring frequently, until it is smooth and glossy. The sauce should thinly coat the back of the spoon.

4 Stir in the cream and a little salt and black pepper and heat gently to warm through.

PESTO

PESTO IS QUICK AND EASY TO MAKE IN A FOOD PROCESSOR, BUT IF YOU DON'T HAVE ONE, TRYING BLENDING THE INGREDIENTS, IN SMALL BATCHES, USING AN IMMERSION BLENDER. FRESHLY MADE PESTO HAS NUMEROUS USES, MOST COMMONLY AS A PASTA SAUCE BUT ALSO TO FLAVOR SOUPS, STEWS, AND RISOTTOS.

1 Tear the basil into pieces and put into a food processor or blenderwith the pine nuts, Parmesan, and garlic.

2 Blend lightly until the nuts and cheese are broken into small pieces, scraping the mixture down from the sides of the bowl, if necessary.

3 Add the olive oil and a little salt and blend to a thick paste. Stir into freshly cooked pasta or turn into a bowl and refrigerate. It can be kept, covered, for up to 5 days.

1 cup basil, including stems
⅓ cup pine nuts
1 cup grated vegetarian
  Parmesan-style cheese
2 garlic cloves, chopped
½ cup olive oil
salt

Serves 4
Prep time 5 minutes

To make Red Pesto, drain 1 cup sun-dried tomatoes in oil, chop them into small pieces, and add to the food processor instead of the basil.

APPLESAUCE

THE SECRET OF A GOOD APPLESAUCE IS TO USE PLENTY OF BUTTER AND LET THE APPLES AND FLAVORINGS COOK SLOWLY.

4 tablespoons unsalted butter
3 large cooking apples, peeled, cored, and chopped
¼ cup sugar
6 whole cloves
finely grated zest and juice of 1 lemon
salt

1 Melt the butter in a heavy saucepan. Add the apples, sugar, cloves, lemon zest and juice, and a little salt.

2 Cover the pan with a lid and let cook gently over the lowest heat for about 20 minutes, stirring the mixture occasionally, until the apples are soft and mushy. Adjust the seasoning, adding a little more lemon juice for a tangier flavor, if desired. Transfer to a bowl and serve warm or cold.

Serves 6
Prep time **10 minutes**
Cooking time **20 minutes**

GLOSSY CHOCOLATE SAUCE

USE A GOOD-QUALITY BITTERSWEET CHOCOLATE TO GIVE THIS SAUCE A RICH FLAVOR AND PLENTY OF SHEEN. BE CAREFUL TO AVOID OVERHEATING THE CHOCOLATE OR THE SAUCE WILL DEVELOP A GRAINY TEXTURE.

¾ cup sugar
8 oz semisweet chocolate, chopped
2 tablespoons unsalted butter

1 Put the sugar into a small, heavy saucepan and add ½ cup of water. Cook over low heat, stirring constantly with a wooden spoon, until the sugar has dissolved.

2 Bring the syrup to a boil and boil for 1 minute, then remove the pan from the heat and let cool for 1 minute. Add the chocolate to the pan.

3 Add the butter and let stand until the chocolate and butter have melted, stirring frequently, until the sauce is smooth and glossy. If the last of the chocolate doesn't melt completely or you want to serve the sauce warm, return the pan briefly to the lowest heat setting.

Serves 5-6
Prep time **5 minutes**
Cooking time **2-3 minutes**

1 stick unsalted butter, softened
1¼ cups confectioners' sugar

Makes enough for a 7-8 inch cake
Prep time **3 minutes**

Buttercream

THE BEST BUTTERCREAM IS SOFT AND FLUFFY WITH A FLAVOR THAT'S NOT TOO OVERPOWERINGLY SWEET.

1 Beat the butter in a bowl with a little of the sugar until smooth.

2 Add the remaining sugar and beat until pale and fluffy. Add a few drops of boiling water and beat for another few moments.

For a coffee-flavor alternative, dissolve 1 tablespoon instant espresso powder in 2 teaspoons boiling water and beat into the buttercream.

Cream Cheese FROSTING

THIS IS A WONDERFUL TANGY FROSTING WITH PLENTY OF FLAVOR, AND IT'S GREAT FOR ANYONE WHO DOESN'T LIKE INTENSELY SUGARY SPREADS. TASTE FOR SWEETNESS ONCE IT'S WHISKED—YOU CAN EASILY BEAT IN ANOTHER 3 TABLESPOONS OF SUGAR IF IT'S NOT SWEET ENOUGH.

1 cup cream cheese
1-2 teaspoons lime juice or lemon juice
⅔ cup confectioners' sugar

1 Beat the cream cheese in a bowl until it is softened and smooth. Beat in 1 teaspoon of the juice.

2 Add the confectioners' sugar and beat until smooth, adding a little more juice if the mixture is firm.

Makes enough for a 7-8 inch cake
Prep time **3 minutes**

INDEX

ACKNOWLEDGMENTS

Picture Credits
Octopus Publishing Group Stephen Conroy
72, 93, 95, 97, 101, 102, 104, 131, 145, 149, 151, 187,
203, 204, 215, 218, 222, 225, 228, 231, 236, 238,
245, 249; Will Heap 11, 26, 53, 64, 109, 110, 113,
122, 123, 130, 133, 134, 138, 139, 193, 200, 210,
217; William Lingwood 213; David Munns 219,
233; Lis Parsons 68, 147, 239, 242 above;
William Reavell 17, 29, 33, 39, 40, 44, 49, 55, 57,
85, 105, 111, 115, 140, 154, 155, 157, 161, 163, 169,
174, 177, 181, 183, 191, 196, 221, 227; Gareth
Sambidge 16, 62, 63, 87, 229; William Shaw 13,
15, 23, 27, 28, 37, 41, 43, 47, 61, 67, 71, 75, 81, 83,
84, 89, 90, 98, 103, 119, 125, 127, 135, 152, 158,
159, 167, 171, 173, 188, 195, 205, 211, 242 below;
Ian Wallace 19, 22, 46, 56, 86, 91, 128, 189, 198,
201, 223; **Shutterstock** Anneka 136; Beauty
photographer 74; BlueOrange Studio 21 above;
cluckva 14 background; designelements 87
background; Gencho Petkov 47 background;
Goran Bogicevic 5 above; HLPhoto 51 below;
Martin Parratt 179 below; MShev 137; Nejron
Photo 4 below, 20, 240; pcruciatti 179 above;
pepmibastock 3 background; photastic 12
background, 81 background; primopiano 65
background; Quanthem 21 below; taviphoto 79
background; The_Pixel 10 background; vetkit 2
background; worker 16 background; YanLev 3
below; Yulia Davidovich 51 above, 178; Zeljko
Bozic 180 background. **Thinkstock** Hemera
Technologies 31 background; kyoshino 4
background; Milos Luzanin 18 background;
Nastco 32 background.

Publisher Sarah Ford
Editor Pauline Bache
Features Writer Cara Frost-Sharratt
Designers Eoghan O'Brien and Jaz Bahra
Picture Library Manager Jennifer Veall
Assistant Production Controller
Meskerem Berhane